Freelancer

*Become your own boss
within the Hair and
Beauty Industry*

By April. C

"I am an optimist; I believe in living life on purpose but also in the power to create the kind of life we desire by focusing on goals and taking action."

– *April.C*

Contact the author

april@aprilwritesbooks.com

@freelancer_hair_beauty_book

CONTENTS

FOREWORD

HAS FREELANCING CHANGED my life? Oh yes! Was it easy? Oh no! I've made two attempts to succeed as a freelancer in my life. Neither time was easy, but my second try was undoubtedly easier and successful because I was ready!

If you're expecting to read a book from someone earning seven figures or who is internationally recognized in the hair and beauty industry (HBI), I want to stop you right there. This book will not be what you expect; I am not someone you can't relate to.

This book is for all people who are a part of my world: the hair and beauty sector.

Do you wonder if this book is for you?

If you are a beauty expert wondering whether or not to take the leap and become a freelancer, yes, this book is for you.

If you are a freelancer already but feel that something is overlooked, this book will help you level up your game.

The freelancer lifestyle is trendy nowadays. Many hair and beauty experts are quitting their full-time jobs to jump into this lifestyle of freedom.

- But, is it the right time for you?
- Do you understand all the pros and cons of working on your own?
- Do you have any idea where to start from?
- Do you know your options?

Probably not. Like all of us when beginning our freelancing journey.

This book will give you a better understanding of the big picture and the commitment levels required. It aims to give you the tools to make decisions on purpose and grow your idea with confidence by overcoming all the questions, fears, emotions, and doubts. *Freelancer* is your chance to learn from someone who's done it all already - made the mistakes and learned the lessons!

In this book, you will find personal experiences combined with helpful information and resources on the hair and beauty industry. I will also explain to you what led me to choose this lifestyle twice—why the first time it didn't work out and why the second time it did.

Setting up your own business and starting this exciting new adventure can also be overwhelming; some situations are challenging, and they may discourage you.

Let's get you ready by setting up your expectations; I want you to kick off your new journey in the smoothest way. If you like the idea of being a freelancer and if you are willing to build a plan—you could start working on your dream right now!

Becoming a freelancer is the best thing that happened to my career.

I trained as a hairdresser over 16 years ago, and I've been lucky enough to gain experience in various positions. I was raised in a business; I worked in hair and beauty salons with different business models; some people would say that I was more successful when I occupied an important position and managed up to 70 people. But, you know, being a freelancer, I have never felt more fulfiled, so I will share my story with you to help you understand where this feeling comes from.

Running a hair salon has never been my dream; however, I am way too independent to work for somebody else. It might be about standards, but I am not ready to compromise — not anymore.

The desire to start your business is a big move; it does not just happen; there are always triggers. Have you identified yours yet?

Triggers can be silly, such as being fed up with filling out forms asking for permission to go on holiday, or choosing the clients and brands you want to work with. However, triggers can even be more than this: maybe the desire of improving your clients' experience is driving you, or perhaps you'd like to spend as long as needed on your clients without hearing about targets?

Unfortunately, triggers can get more profound and dramatic, such as leaving a toxic work environment, redundancy, or giving up on a promised pay rise that never arrived. Sound familiar?

When I set up my first business, I doubted my decisions every single time because I did not have the answers to all my questions. I wish I had a book like this one when I had sleepless nights trying to figure out if freelancing could help me to build the work-life balance I really needed.

You cannot set up your business without first considering its chances of success. I will explain how to do this and, I will also give you some tools to weigh the risks; you need to know your options!

To clarify, I don't want to convince you that freelancing is the best and only way to live happily as a hair or beauty expert. The HBI offers a vast range of beautiful and extraordinary career paths; however, if freelancing is the way you want to go, let's raise your awareness to overcome stress and make your decision an educated one.

You are not alone.

I have been working crazy and exhausting hours since the first day of my career. I ran up to 12 businesses, I had two massive burnouts, and today I am co-owner and co-founder of a small business in another industry while also being a very proud member of the HBI freelancing community. I trained as a hairdresser and nail artist, but this book can help anyone within the HBI.

This book's technical parts have been written alongside professionals; they are experts working with me and my businesses daily.

I hope this book will help and guide you and as many hair and beauty experts as possible. In life and at work, you totally deserve self-fulfilment, happiness, and over everything, freedom.

ARE YOU READY?

Part 1

THE GOOD REASON

We all have a good reason to take the leap.

There is always a trigger.

This is how I became a freelancer.

MY HAIRDRESSING JOURNEY started when I was thirteen. My family moved to a small village in the French Alps; it was surrounded by mountains and not far from the famous ski stations Courchevel and Meribel.

My bedroom faced a 200-year-old historic castle and a hair salon. This house was very charming, all constructed out of stone—yet at that time, I already knew I would not live the rest of my life there. My family and I lived on the house's first floor, and the ground floor was my parents' pastry shop (I know, SO French, SO cliché! But hey… SO good!)

It was in this pastry shop that I had my very first job. My parents were (and still are) working extremely hard six days a week, providing fresh and tasty bread, pastries, and chocolates - everything that makes you happy… and chubby!

In 2022, it will be the 20th anniversary of their business. If you ask my parents their secrets for a long-lasting company, they will tell you: "Sacrifice, hard work, and consistency." In my opinion, it is insane and unhealthy to work so hard and for so long, but in the end, it is all about choice: when you are running your own business, it is part of your freedom of choice, and nobody should judge you for your choices.

I worked at my parents' shop every weekend, after school, on Wednesday afternoons, school holidays . . . I was not very happy at the time, but it taught me so much! I moaned a lot, and my mum used to say, "Come on! Put a smile on your face; the clients don't have to see how grumpy you are today!" So, with my most beautiful smile on, I stepped into the shop: "Bonjour!…"

There, it was all about the client experience: a lesson I learned for life!

My father shared so much with me. While he made the bread every night for the following day, I stood with him, leaning against the wall, and we chatted for hours. I thought at the time that these were just regular conversations; however, my father was giving me the tools and confidence to run my own business—I wonder if he realised?

Growing up as a teenager in my parents' business was an interesting experience; every day was a lesson, if you were prepared to look for it and learn from it. Some employees were late, another stole cash from the till; I saw my mum expertly manage difficult customers; and I was taught how to cash up a till and create a float for the next working day. These were all valuable lessons. I guess the way a business works just becomes a regular thing - like cooking pasta - and in the end, it's something you feel able to do with confidence. Did this help when I started my first freelance company? Yes, but it certainly didn't give me all the tools to succeed as a freelancer.

My results were not brilliant at school. I had a rigorous education, but all I wanted was to have fun! So, I was this "rest on her achievements" and "does not exploit her potential" girl. I believe that we all have potential, we just need to decide whether to use it or not. Sometimes we are not ready to unlock it as a teen but as an adult, we can strive for it.

At 13, we had to do an internship in a business. The goal was to help us choose a career path to determine what we wanted to do for the rest of our lives! This still shocks me. You're expected to decide what you want to do and who you want to be for the rest of your life. How can we choose a career path at 13 or 14 years old? How can you decide if you want to study or learn a manual job?

So many of my friends were pushed by their parents to graduate from university. In the end, they went for beautician, or hairdresser training. "Choose a job you love, and you will never have to work a day in your life," Confucius once said. True or not, I particularly love the HBI because you can jump in anytime; the rules are yours, and your professional background does not matter.

Secretly, I wanted to become a lawyer but there were no lawyers in my small village, with no option to commute to the city. So, I just took the most straightforward opportunity and knocked on the door of the hair salon next door. When you were not very good at school, and when your results were not enough to get to high college, they would send you to learn manual jobs.

In my case, my teachers disagreed on the hairdressing education path I wanted to follow. They stated that it would "waste my potential." Nonsense. I feel very blessed now that my parents valued the HBI. They fought for me to let me do what I wanted. At the time, I remember the teachers seeing this industry as an "alternative path" to college, to "at least gain some easy qualifications," your kind of last chance to do something with your life. Sad.

I chose this job at random and, luckily, I fell in love with it.

The HBI is constantly evolving and changing, and our industry is finally perceived differently. We are not JUST hairdressers or beauty therapists; we are skilled, cultivated, and educated professionals. We impact people's lives and sometimes earn as much as people in "high status" corporate roles. After I joined it, all those years ago, I saw for myself what so many are wrong about: the HBI is not an "alternative career" or "last chance" industry. I am so proud of it — as much as you probably are too!

After my internship, the salon was where I spent all my weekends and holidays until the age of sixteen—working for free! I will never forget the feeling; it was such a happy place. It smelt so good and felt so cosy; a client would enter, receive a beauty service while laughing, gossiping and drinking before leaving beautiful and confident. I wanted to be in a hair salon for the rest of my life!

Do you remember what you felt when you spent your first day in a salon?

When the time arrived, my parents paid for a private school for me to qualify and graduate, as, in France, you cannot legally work without a diploma. I will be forever grateful for those four years of full-time training.

Back then, I was in love with pink hair. I loved the smell of the "Alchemic Silver Mask" from the brand "Davines" and even gave my mum chunky blonde and copper highlights!

I learned all the styling basics including perms, rolls, classic updos, and finger waves (which I hope won't be a trend again too soon!) However, I really believe that we should all learn all the fundamentals of our job, every detail! What is a building with weak foundations? So, when you start working for yourself, make sure you know your basics—unless you specialise in something particular.

I was lucky enough to get contracted to style the hair of a Burberry guest during a London Fashion Week—an opportunity that I got being a freelancer, by the way! When I saw the mood board included finger waves, I mentally thanked my teachers for my education!

If you especially desire to be involved in events and fashion shows, your basics are everything—and if you don't know them, learn and train—this is key! Fashion is a giant wheel. Several decades ago, the mullet was born and became a trend for little while; years later, in 2020, the mullet made its come-back, and this hairstyle is trendier than ever.

Experience and education in the HBI are your best assets - which makes even more sense as a freelancer.

When I started my diploma, I was so passionate about hair! Do you remember feeling like an absolute workaholic at the very beginning of your career? I felt like a *hairaholic*—I recall this adrenalin and hunger to learn and create—such a powerful feeling!

Years later, I must admit that this passion tarnished over time; if you work in a beauty salon/clinic, you probably know what I mean.

You often work on targets, multitasking under strict timings while providing the BEST service and experience possible! As a result, your passion can diminish because you feel drained and overworked. It makes it hard to find the energy to train or improve your skills.

I fell in love with my job all over again when I became a freelancer.

When I am tired, I have chosen it, it is even rewarding, and I always make time for what is important—thanks to a flexible schedule. I now have time to train and love what I do again.

Two years after I graduated, I started straight away with a second degree to become fully qualified. I worked two days a week at school and three days a week in a hair salon. This is how I started working in a chain located in a mall.

It must be because I've been brought up in a business, but when I visit a restaurant or work somewhere, I like to analyse, and compare business models.

The managerial side of any business has always fascinated me. Although sometimes it's unconscious, I try to learn from people's behaviour, leadership, branding, clients' attitude, and team communication to understand how that business works and makes money. To understand their marketing strategy, I try to recall what made me want to go to their business and how I heard about them.

To me, a business is like watching a movie and trying to define the role of every protagonist. So, wherever you are working at the moment, or if you are going to any shop today, whatever its size or industry, I encourage you to look at it from a business point of view:

- What do you see?
- How does it make you feel?
- How does the experience feel?
- Pay attention; it's so inspiring!

Later, I decided to train and work as a nail artist alongside my hairdressing job. This is where my first freelance company was born. Then I moved to the South of France, which I now consider home.

I kept doing nails, I started my business from scratch again, with a new clientele, I worked based at a fascinating place.

This hair and beauty salon was run by two men in their late 50s; their brand and reputation attracted demanding and wealthy clients with a very posh style attitude. Some clients used to park their yacht in front of the hair salon like you would park your bicycle. So far from my reality!

Providing nail services in this salon was very difficult. I remember a client asking me the colour of the inner lining of a 2.55 Chanel handbag, "You know from the 60s, darling!" I had no idea what a Chanel bag, or any designer bag for that matter, looked like!

She said, "If you don't show me the colour now, I'm not getting my nails done with you." This woman was clearly trying to challenge me, and her attitude was not acceptable. Unfortunately, however, it was permitted in the salon I worked in; a shame, right?

This day I promised myself that any business I would create in the future would never tolerate this kind of behaviour. If your clients keep behaving in a certain and inappropriate manner, this is because you let them.

I really wanted to open the door for her and get her out of my sight, but the salon owner gave that look and discretely pointed out a dark red bottle of shampoo. I understood that the inner lining of that annoying bag was burgundy — OF COURSE!

When working with the public, you must be ready to expect any kind of client. I learned with time that the brand and management scheme sets the rules and boundaries, and it applies to the smallest business, including your freelance business.

A lesson learned for life!

Another beautiful side to working as a freelancer is that you get to choose who you want to work with.

The owners of this salon I worked in were two wealthy Parisians. They ran a few famous salons in Paris in the 70s, but after being robbed and assaulted twice at home, they decided to sell their salons and moved to the South of France.

I have always seen them as fashion icons (although, at that time, I had no idea about fashion). Their clients were very much like them because their brand reflected their personality. It was not hard for them to satisfy their clients— "what you see is what you get." They proved to me how authenticity is essential in business.

Both men were also very professional, picky, and had precise ideas of what was attractive and what was not.

The two owners would always tell stories and scandals that happened at their Parisian hair salon; people loved it. They would share lessons from their professional education: a strict, bossy, and painful experience, where they had to push themselves extremely hard to get a sufficient look from their boss. I wish this management model had disappeared by now, but even in 2021, it seems to still be a thing. So why don't we refuse to be treated that way? Let's raise our standards, people, whatever our experience, we are human and deserve kindness and respect over everything else, let's acknowledge that we don't have to suffer to succeed.

Watching this kind of "show" was fascinating and kept me entertained for a little while, even when I started to miss doing hair. But unfortunately, summer doing nails for many English tourists signed my end—I didn't speak English, and doing nails was not my thing.

One day, while at work, I received a call from a hair salon owner: "Hello, I am calling you because I was given your number; I need you to work for me, can we meet?"

Do you believe in destiny?

This opportunity led me to take over the management of a group of 12 salons. At the same time, our founder flew to the other side of the world to set up a resort, leaving me on my own, with the help of two extraordinary accountants working for the company full time.

Now, this could have been the end of the story! A gorgeous house along the beach, a few stunning cars, family and friends around me, a fantastic partner: reading this book, wherever you are in the world, you can imagine the social expectations at this point, right? To marry, have kids, plus a dog or two (why not?) and keep living this socially expected life forever.

My ultimate career goal was to manage a group of salons and it felt that at 25 I achieved it way before the end of my career. Did this mean it was the end of the game?

I used to get some remarks from people that would twist my gut:

"You are so young! You have achieved so much!"

"Wow, you are so successful; you must be so happy!"

"Now that your career is successful, what's the next step? Baby? Marriage?"

Well, I lived a stable and established life; this is what people could see from an external point of view.

If Instagram had existed, my grid would have been filled with ME in my fancy car going to work, but also ME at a business lunch in a trendy restaurant on the beach. And why not ME training the teams, or ME after work enjoying BBQs with my amazing friends.

Title, position, material . . . people look at you and just assume. The reality is, I was suffocating.

If Instagram had existed then, I would never have posted about ME and my guilt about firing a manager for blurry reasons under the lead of my boss. Or ME fighting with a stylist because she was drunk and lost it in front of clients.

Absolutely not!

I would certainly never have posted my tired face when my boss would call me at inappropriate hours because of the time difference!

We sometimes feel bad about complaining and telling the truth on social media or in real life. We don't want to look ungrateful and weak, do we? My boss was not from the beauty industry; he just loved a woman and invested in her industry. I learned that uneducated management could work for some time; however, when the foundations are not strong, the business suffers in the long term, and, at some point, it's coming right back for you and strikes you.

Laws and rules are not to be ignored in France or any country!

For example, by law, the timetable had to be displayed within the business and signed by employees - a procedure not applied. Following an argument with the owner, a girl took the business to court and pretended she worked more than she was paid for. Without the timetable signed, the company was not complying with the law and not protected, and so they lost the case. The company lost thousands of euros.

Later, in another business, a client had a hair dye allergic reaction. Although she was a regular client, the compulsory skin test had not been updated, it just happened, and she claimed money for it.

Therefore, when you are building up your own business, whatever it is, a small business or a multinational company, you must make sure to comply with the law.

This applies to freelancers too. Don't be naive thinking that your clients would never do this. This is the only way to protect you, your clients, and your business.

That job provided me with immense pride. It taught me so much and brought me so many joys. However, it was a necessary experience but not a lifelong position.

I loved learning about management, HR, marketing, and more. But, beyond business, what I enjoyed the most was training the teams. Helping people grow was very satisfying!

Still, the reality was that I was constantly under pressure, my standards were high, and so was the pressure I inflicted upon myself. Responsibilities also mean nasty tasks and sleepless nights, no matter how confident or experienced you are.

The pressure was not more bearable in a sunny climate. In life, I had everything, yet it felt as if I had nothing. One night I came back home; I was 25 and exhausted. In the dark, I sat on my sofa, my partner came back from work and found me in tears— that day I didn't have a bad day, everything went smoothly; however, I could not process why I was crying and feeling so miserable. I had no power or strength to keep going.

We will all agree, this is not normal behaviour. That was burnout number one.

With my partner, we talked about a "Plan B" all night long. This is why surrounding yourself with the right people is vital; whatever happens to you in life, they will support you and find a way to uplift you.

Deep down, one part of me wanted to quit this job. I needed a change and I wanted to get back more time for myself. Another part of me was scared to leave this job, to leave comfort, to leave a social status.

Social status feeds your ego, but it does not fulfil your soul. Whatever our job, we always think that happiness is somewhere with a higher status. A stylist intends to be a manager; a manager wants to own the salon; the salon owner aims to run multiple businesses. We always want more, we want to elevate our status in other people's eyes, we want financial security, and if possible, we want everything.

Social status and career growth comes with a price, and it will always impact another area of our life; therefore we must define our priorities. Sometimes, a manager will be more fulfilled as an assistant manager because they won't compromise their family life. For me, freelancing has been the perfect compromise; to say that I am happier as a freelancer than when I ran 12 businesses is an understatement.

People often look at those who have higher status with envy, thinking they must live their best lives. However, nothing comes for free. Elevated status, high income, responsibilities; it all comes in a sparkly package including constant pressure, tremendous amount of work, and very little headspace. Anybody occupying this kind of position will tell you about the sacrifices behind the title.

Funny enough, I always thought that I would never be able to have it all: running my business, earning good money, limiting the responsibilities, and enjoying total freedom. Today, being a freelancer proves to me that I was totally wrong.

If you are a business owner reading this book, you may be considering letting go of the pressures and responsibilities and maybe start freelancing. If it's what you need, going freelance won't be a step back but a step up.

If you are not enjoying your job, or if it does not contribute to your happiness or, even worse, drags you down and makes you feel miserable, it might be the right time to make a change. Sometimes we are so driven by success that we would never quit a high position. But why not? Is it for your ego? For money? What if it would make you happy again? Time taught me that quitting a job is not a failure. In fact, if it leads you to new experiences, happiness, and fulfilment, it is a massive win!

Whatever your social status and position, you are responsible for your own choices and your life. There are always alternatives. Build your PLAN B! We have the power to create the kind of life we want by focusing on goals and taking action. Why keep a job just for the sake of it?

Money is essential - but is it everything? From my point of view, it is not. Money is not what makes you happy anyway.

I personally decided to bury my ego deep down in my pocket. I made the choice to ignore my doubts, the social norms, and people's expectations. I chose happiness and fulfilment over status and ego. Four months later, my partner and I moved to London.

We swapped our pretty house along the beach for a horrendous house share, and I worked for five years in a private and busy hair salon in London. I learned English, worked out the methods and secrets of British hairdressing, and built up a business from scratch in another industry with my partner. On the way, I met new people and made friends for life. Today, I would not have it any other way—when you fight so hard to get something, you cherish it even more.

Five hard years later, after building a life from scratch, I burnt out again. Burnout is a real phenomenon today, but sadly talking about it can be taboo. It might be uncomfortable if we talk about being overworked, anxious, or unhappy; we might worry about sounding weak or feeling like a failure. But acknowledging it and sharing your feelings with someone you trust or a professional really helps.

At burnout #1, when I was tired, I kept unpacking my feelings to my boss. He used to tell me, "You just need a holiday." But I needed much more than that. I was in a state of emotional, physical, and mental exhaustion caused by years of excessive work and prolonged stress that spilled over all areas of my life and caused my downfall.

When burnout #2 happened, it hit me hard!

You must be thinking, OMG, a second one? How did you not learn the first time? But, when you are driven and enjoy what you do, I realise that a very fine line keeps you from comprehending when you are doing too much, and it's easy to cross it.

Where is the line? Especially when working on clients, it feels so good to create and give to people. Also, growing a business feels fantastic when you start seeing the results of your hard work, but that can become quite addictive…

I remember that I had no inspiration anymore; I couldn't even make simple choices like choosing between an apple or a banana. I even had inflammation marks on my face: every day was a bad day. I jumped from an achievement to another without feeling anything, not even joy or satisfaction. I was just tired everyday, all day.

When I reflect on this time, it felt like I went from climbing a mountain, living extremely happily on top of it for a short time, then, from one day to another, slowly falling from it until suddenly I was collapsed in a heap at the bottom. I was unhappy, with no strength to attempt climbing it again.

This second burnout happened because I did not set boundaries. Driven by my ambitions, I chose to overwork, and in doing so, disrespected my well-being. I didn't delegate work enough; I would work into the night and wake up at 4am to achieve more. I would invest my energy anywhere and everywhere, even where it was not profitable.

What an apparent mistake in hindsight, right?

In fact, when you are unhappy, you cannot make your clients happy. Your clients feel the negative vibes as well as the positive ones.

You cannot pretend to be yourself when you feel exhausted and dead inside.

You cannot provide the best experience to your clients if you are not your best self.

Writing about my burnouts is very important to me because I want you to raise your awareness.

Becoming a freelancer involves having a lot on your plate: setting new routines, admin, clients ... the list goes on. If you're wondering (as I once did) where the line is, let me tell you: YOU are drawing it! You are the only person responsible for drawing the line in your career - a line of boundaries, self-care, and respect.

Here comes my best tip for you: you need to build up a healthy and sustainable lifestyle for yourself from day one. Even if you decide not to start a business, drawing this line is crucial for anyone.

When you are freelancing, you represent your business. Depending on your previous experiences the pressure can be high and overwhelming. One day, you may have to say "no." "No," for example, to a client booking last minute who wants to be "fitted in." To say "NO" might feel heart-breaking, but don't you think that your 7pm client deserves as much energy and love as your 8am client? After all, they are paying the same price. Do you think it is humanly possible to provide the same amount of energy after 11 hours of work?

I learned along the way to re-evaluate my priorities: my well-being is my priority, I set boundaries, and I have learned to say no. Of course, there are a few exceptions, and life happens, but for me, it is now occasional, not a daily occurrence anymore.

Another thing I have learned is to nourish my creative side. Creativity is so powerful and, from the words of my meditation teacher, is "one of the best antidotes to fight stress, anxiety and avoid burn out." It is essential for us to experience new things, enjoy our hobbies and have fun. Implementing regular time for relaxation in your weekly routine is also a powerful way to reset and let go. Yoga and mediation are excellent ways to clear up your mind, recharge your energy, and release stress.

Since I built up a healthy lifestyle for myself, allowing for plenty of sleep, healthy food, and time off from technology, I feel energised and far more productive. In addition, I can rest assured knowing that this routine will keep me sustained in the long run. It is all about time management; you book your clients for services, so why not book yourself for self-care? I am not going to experience burnout #3!

Learning about mindfulness will give you the *best* chance to live your *best* life and be your *best* self!

Yes, burnouts happen. They can happen to anyone; however, we shouldn't fear them or deliberately not accept opportunities. Burnouts sometimes must happen for us to learn, so if you reassess, rest, and reset before restarting, you'll come out the other side stronger and ready for anything!

When burnout #2 happened, I decided to make a move to become a freelancer again. I had thousands of doubts; everything felt very confused. If the *Freelancer Starter Checklist* Part 8 of this book had existed, it would have been a game-changer. It's so much easier when somebody who has done it before you gives you direction.

Every freelancer has a story; some were lucky and had time to prep their freelancing journey.

Some others have been thrown into this new adventure without notice, and it was a survival matter.

We are not all equal, but let's not forget that we all belong to the same industry and community. So never fear to ask why people started their freelancing journey and how they made it; you will be amazed by how inspiring and relatable it can be; which is sometimes the ultimate push of motivation you need to seriously consider this big move.

Part 2

THE HAIR AND BEAUTY INDUSTRY. WHAT TO EXPECT?

WHEN YOU STEP into any industry, it is essential to understand it.

Official definitions of the HBI include hair washing, trimming, and cutting, setting, dyeing, tinting, waving, straightening, barbering, shaving and beard trimming, trichology, facial massage, manicure and pedicure, makeup, electrolysis, and other beauty treatments; but not the manufacture of wigs.[*]

I look at the HBI and see this massive bubble of creative people. This industry has just so much to offer, and there are so many ways to be part of it. Of course, you could work as a hairstylist, beautician, or nail technician. However, there are

[*] Source NHBF and the data source

also many job opportunities in businesses that allow and power the industry to be what it is, such as manufacturers, distributors, suppliers, salons, schools, education companies, magazines, and much more!

Due to the global pandemic, our industry is suffering and will suffer for a little while. The lockdown impact has been brutal — loss of income, psychological pressure, and physical pressure to work on and off. None of this has been easy or expected, and it is a lot to digest and overcome.

In December 2020, the British Beauty Council reported that since the pandemic in March 2020, "4,578 hair and beauty salons up and down the country in the UK closed their doors for good."

A lot of hair and beauty salons are closed and are still closing. All around the world, this pandemic is ruining businesses and leaving business owners with debts and broken dreams.

During this crisis, freelancers have been particularly hard hit. Of course, every country functions differently, however during lockdowns, those working for themselves didn't have employee benefits, such as sick pay or the furlough scheme, and not everybody could get a grant. Tough times.

However, it is essential to highlight that the way the industry has faced the situation was exceptional; social media was full of love and support for the industry. The hair and beauty community were active, raising awareness, sharing important information, and spreading love and hope.

Even individually, people came up with unique ideas to become greener, sell online, teach . . . Amazing online classes were available at discounted rates (some were even free!), providing skills and confidence to communities before preparing to go back to work.

Some freelance businesses were born during the lockdown. The generosity that people have shown each other is mind-blowing! In the end, we all went through it as a community with support and kindness.

As a freelancer, this is something you want to know; whatever happens, you are not alone; the hair and beauty industry has a vast, strong, and active community.

In the UK, the NHBF (National Hair and Beauty Federation) has even announced that the Government has created a new sector for hair and beauty called "Personal Care" dedicated to support our industry and raise awareness to the world outside it.

Of course, you might wonder if planning to start a business in unprecedented times is a good idea; in that case, it is more important now than ever to conduct extensive research and seek as much professional and personal advice as possible. In fact, this crisis is affecting all of us not just as a society but as individuals, too. Our clients' behaviour and ways of living and spending money have changed. People might space out their appointments and spread them differently due to traveling again and working from home. Therefore, you need to understand how it will impact your future business, and meticulous calculations are necessary.

If your dream is to be part of this industry as a freelancer, if deep down you know it's where you're meant to be, give yourself a chance. Do not let the world madness steal your dreams. This beautiful industry still has so much to offer and still needs every single one of us!

"Have great hopes and dare to go all out for them. Have great dreams and dare to live them. Have tremendous expectations and believe in them."

– Norman Vincent Peale

Evolution and competition challenge

The HBI is an ever-growing industry! New trends, new products on the market, new techniques, and scientific discoveries. It can be overwhelming as all of this happens so fast, especially since the dawn of social media. With so many talented people on Instagram, it can sometimes feel overcrowded, like there's no space for anyone else, especially you.

In fact, when you are considering setting up your own business, the main challenge in this industry is that it can feel very competitive — hair and beauty salons are trading on just about every corner. So, although we cannot see mobile freelancers, they still count!

The good thing about competition is that it drives us to be the best we can be. It takes us out of our comfort zone and forces us to provide better services, creating room for growth. And at the end, where there is competition, there is a lucrative market.

We must keep in mind that the world is changing, and so is our clientele. Consumers of yesterday are not the same ones of tomorrow. Some factors that are important to consider are:

- Psychological (motivation, perception, learning, beliefs, and attitudes)
- Personal (age and life-cycle stage, occupation, economic circumstances, lifestyle, personality, and self-concept)
- Social (reference groups, family, roles, and status)
- Cultural (culture, subculture, social class system)

As humans, we are always seeking change and innovations, and so are our customers. So, it is not only about creating your business just to get clients in; it is also about striving to keep them loyal time after time.

I remember a hairdresser where I used to work. She was very experienced, but her work was a long way off being up to the salon's standards; post balayage service, if a client had bleach patches, it was her client. Also, her haircuts were far from being the best; it sounds terrible, I know, but you know what? Her column was fully booked every day. It was impossible not to notice this woman; she had an incredible vibe. I still remember her great attitude and contagious smile, and clients requested her every time. Her energy was fascinating!

I am not saying that you can succeed even with poor skills. What I mean is that you might be excellent at what you do, however, the competition is tough, and in the end, what will last is the experience. The brain remembers emotion, which is why clients will come back to you instead of somebody else. Emotion acts like a highlighter, emphasising certain aspects of experiences to make them more memorable.

Competition is a stress point when you are doubting yourself. Imagine the idea of failing or being left behind. It can be terrifying!

Equally (and strangely), we can also fear success. Do you? People fear success because IF they succeed, there will be pressure to maintain that success, and if they don't, this may lead to failure. As humans, we might fear failure because we fear it might define us.

Does failure define people?
NO, OF COURSE NOT!

The reality is that we are ultimately competing with ourselves; our greatest adversary is our own ego.

At a fundamental level, our ego desires to live in a place where everything goes our way and where struggles do not exist; you know, an effortless and unrealistic life. But, despite all our learning, there will always be room for improvement.

So, let's focus and get ready to fight our fears.

"I've learned that people will forget what you said, people will forget what you did, but people will never forget how you made them feel."

———————

– Maya Angelou

Nobody is you.

This is your strength.

You are special.

Your uniqueness is your secret and ultimate weapon.

You are enough.

Be kind.

Be generous.

Show love for your clients.

Care.

Focus on what your clients need.

Always go the extra mile.

Be yourself.

Shine.

Fly.

Do not let fear get the better of you, believe in yourself, and overcome this competition anxiety.

Our deepest fear is not that
we are inadequate.
Our deepest fear is that
we are powerful beyond
measure.
It is our light, not our
darkness that most
frightens us.

_____

– *Nelson Mandela*

Part 3

FREELANCING

THE FREELANCER'S LIFESTYLE is very trendy now. The crazy concept of setting your own salary and deciding whether to work or not sounds quite dreamy and, the fact is, you can be a freelancer in any industry.

Freelancer is a term commonly used for a person who is self-employed and not necessarily committed to a particular long-term employer.

Essentially, a freelance job is where a person works for themselves rather than for a company. For example, a freelancer can do contract work for different companies and organisations. However, they are ultimately self-employed, provide a service, sell goods, and invoice the client directly.

If you are a freelancer, you are not considered an "employee" by the companies you work for but rather a "contractor." So, you don't get payslips; you invoice other companies and clients. Freelancers can be represented by a company or a temporary agency that works with clients directly; others work independently or use professional associations or websites to get work. They aren't employed by a company or committed to a single customer — freelancers have the freedom to choose the projects they'd like to work on and the clients they'd like to work for.

Freelancing is a smart way of working for those in the creative industries. You may have also heard freelancers being referred to as "self-employed" or "non-staff." There are many words for it, but all these ultimately mean the same thing!

FREELANCING IN THE HBI

As a freelancer in the HBI, the usual arrangement is to rent a chair or a room in a salon. Paying either a membership, a regular flat fee, or a proportion of your earnings to the owner. However, there are new alternatives such as co-working beauty spaces where every individual runs a business within a business.

If you specialise in a field, companies hire freelancers to work on short contracts/missions for events such as theatres, musicals, weddings, or festivals.

The HBI is packed with potential career paths and occupation opportunities.

Specifically, some roles in the HBI are:

Hairstylist

Colourist

Makeup artist

Barber

Skin therapist

Lash specialist

Nail artist

Session stylist

And of course many more...

THE LEGALITIES

Self-employment will always come with its risks but being well-informed on the basics will help you immensely. It obviously varies considering the country or state—if you are in the UK, generally, a freelancer is a self-employed person who:

–   Pays their own income tax, known as self-employment tax.

–   Doesn't usually have employees but may outsource work for specific projects.

–   Has complete control over where they work and their working hours.

The capability to create your own money is one of the utmost sustaining things you can do, and once you get into the stream of functioning, the legal phases will come naturally. Therefore, if you're planning to initiate a profession as a freelancer, you must always consider these three legal necessities for freelancers before you begin:

1.   Register yourself with any one of the certified Tax Authorities where you live. At the culmination of each fiscal year, you'll be required to submit your tax. If you are unable to provide your tax return appropriately, you could be subjected to penalty duties.

2.   Create contracts with your clients - if you are working with companies. That said, a written contract agreement will make the whole process a lot easier and ensure the terms surrounding your work are

clear for both parties. With clients, an estimate or quote will do the job.

3. Buying insurance is also a good idea. Never under-value the significance of insurance.

Even if you work from home, you may need communal accountability insurance as your home-based insurance perhaps won't cover reparations that occur during working hours.

For more information, I would encourage you to check your government's legal freelancer obligations.

Freedom lies in being bold
_____

– Robert Frost

Part 4

BECOMING A FREELANCER

To Freelance or Not to Freelance?

ANYBODY CAN BECOME a freelancer, but is freelancing for everybody? It does not matter if you have six or thirty-years' experience, you must always make sure that you are ready to fly! You are about to create a business, and you need to evaluate its chance of success.

It's about working out the technical details if you aim to live from your income and avoid money loss. You will need complementary skill sets that you'll probably have to learn - nobody was born with all the skills to run a business! To be a wicked boss is a mindset. Allow yourself to reach for the stars!

If you are committed to succeed and surround yourself with the right people, you will more than likely reach your dreams. So, choose the best for yourself and nothing less.

Between stimulus and response, there is a space. In that space is our power to choose our response. In our response lies our growth and our freedom.

————————

– Viktor Emil Frankl
(Austrian neurologist and psychiatrist)

Be brave
Be confident
Be ready to work hard
Be prepared to learn new skills
Be patient
Believe in yourself

Because you will need to:

Build a brand
Market yourself
Manage your clients on your own
Manage the admin side of your business
Be consistent
And more...

COMMON FEARS & FEELINGS

Firstly, there should be no shame surrounding emotions; our feelings are what make us human.

Most of the time, when you decide to go freelance, there is always a trigger, sometimes multiple ones.

What is yours?

Maybe you are unhappy about the business/brand you are working for; you want to create your own business model to finally break the rules and set your own standards.

Maybe you have years of experience, are an expert in your field, and have a loyal clientele. At some point, it might just feel like it's time to experience something new. That's natural.

Maybe you'd love to own a salon, but it is not the right time, and so you are starting off small to test the waters.

Now, I will tell you the truth, the feelings at this stage can be such a rollercoaster! In the beginning, just thinking about the change in your life can be like a big breath of fresh air! Hopefully, you will have fervent supporters around you encouraging and pushing you to take the plunge and do what's best for you. You will already picture yourself running your own business, working with your ideal clients only, not working on Saturdays anymore... that dopamine rushing through your system will be so empowering; it'll feel so good!

Then, super pumped, you are going to start digging into the unknown. You will probably have 1,000 questions about the process. You will begin to do some research, start to doubt, and question yourself, think about the worst, then balance pros and cons, you will try to find the best strategy to quit your job . . . it will start to be overwhelming...WHAT A HEADACHE!

At this very moment, there will probably also be those people—you know the ones—the pessimistic, being slightly less encouraging, pointing out the risks only and talking about the worst. Their impact on you will make you feel anxious, and you might start feeling that starting your business is maybe not the best idea.

Be aware, some people simply don't like change, and they themselves would be petrified to take the leap! When somebody around them does level up, it can act as a mirror to themselves, showing them what they aren't doing. It's all about them and their fears; it's not about you. You don't need these people in your life, let alone when they could sabotage what could be your most important move.

This could potentially affect your confidence and push you to doubt yourself way too much; you will be tempted to step back without even giving yourself a chance.

To make a move is never easy, especially when it is about quitting your job to start your own journey. Even the most popular and talented professionals in the industry are nervous to start their own business: What if I fail? What if I can't put food on the table? What if I can't afford to pay for the school of my children anymore? They are just human feelings that you need to understand to overcome.

I'm telling you, if you don't feel any fear at this point, you could be extraordinarily bold - and maybe dangerously too confident. I promise you that any successful freelancer making it look easy has felt lost and out of their comfort zone when they started freelancing. What makes the difference is your response to the challenge.

Feeling fear and doubt is TOTALLY OKAY.

THE VALUE OF SELF-DOUBT

Self-doubt can be healthy; we are not right all the time and showing humility can help us relate better to others. But we cannot let self-doubt become a state that stops us from moving forward, fearing that something terrible will happen: this is not okay!

Self-doubt is an evil circle. Your background, childhood experiences, or life circumstances impact the way you feel — do not mistake small failures for unworthiness, and do not doubt your qualities. At some point, we all think that we don't measure up, but self-compassion practice and connecting with others can really help.

Let me tell you: you are TOTALLY WORTHY!

SELF-DOUBTING EXPERIENCE/SKILLS

The fear of making mistakes is totally acceptable! If we look at it from another angle, it pushes us in the right direction. If you doubt your experience, it could be a good idea to list your weaknesses to strengths to get back this kick of confidence. You understand your insecurities, but are they rational? Because sometimes they are not. Work on your weaknesses and set realistic expectations for yourself.

Keep learning and build your resilience because, after all, nobody is perfect, and learning is a lifelong achievement.

Anxiety is the dizziness of freedom.

––––––––––

– Søren Kierkegaard,
The Concept of Anxiety

KEY-POINT When going freelance, or changing something important in your life, there is no better time to surround yourself with people who are supportive, love you, and have a positive impact on you—keep them close and hold on tight, as you might be about to make the best choice you have ever made!

FREELANCING PROS AND CONS

Why leave the comfort of an established salon?

This is very personal. There are thousands of reasons out there, and we all have our own unique ones. Belonging to a salon can be very comfortable. But, for some people, after a certain length of time, comfort is not enough.

To question yourself is natural at this stage; it's your survival instinct asking: "WHY? It's so comfy here! Why do you want to expose us to danger?" However, working for someone else means working under their terms and conditions.

With experience, we start to know ourselves. And to become who we want, we need to set our own rules.

Humans have boundaries, and what we at first don't like within a business can become something we cannot bear at all!

The first time I went freelance, I did it with my nail business. I wanted to experience something new and build a plan B to give me options to change jobs. Long story short, I was bored in the hair salon I worked for but mistook this for being bored of hair altogether, so I learned how to do nails. Funnily enough, boredom can push you to do what you have never experienced before just to make you feel alive.

Back then, I had zero experience and built my brand because no nail salons were hiring around me—doing gel on nails was something new at that time. I had no fear as I was not risking anything and kept my other full-time job. I self-funded my project and thanks to my education, I knew what running a big business involved, so a small company with only me seemed easy.

This is also one of the freedoms of freelancing; you can decide to remain a full or part-time employee and you can also freelance in parrallel, providing your employer and your employment contract allows this.

In fact, it gives you the opportunity to do everything you really want to do.

Thanks to our industry's massive diversity, you can also do something different while still connected to the HBI.

When I tried nails, it didn't work out for me because I was not ready (and - importantly - didn't really enjoy doing nails!) I was not thoroughly trained and still had so much to learn. I didn't enjoy working on my own, and without any nail artist community around me, I felt very alone.

TIMING is also vital; it was not the right time for me. I was lucky that the experience didn't affect me emotionally; the risk throughout was relatively low. But if you do take it seriously and hit a wall, this can be very damaging. This could affect your entire life and even your confidence in being your own boss.

Ten years later, I started my second freelance company as I needed the flexibility that no salon would offer me. The trigger also was that double bookings were not something I particularly wanted anymore. Instead, I wanted to provide a different experience for my clients, something more unique and special.

It is always hard to quit a job, but even more so when you appreciate the company owners. You can happen to go through many emotions; you'll probably find that you can be overly hard on yourself, maybe even feeling guilty and ungrateful.

In my case, the business I left allowed me to establish myself in London before I could even speak English. They were as flexible as they could have been with me —they made sure to nurture me, providing education and responsibilities of social media and recruitment. I was so lucky, they took me to Brazil where I spoke in front of 300+ people, then Iceland, Italy . . . They supported me in every single one of my plans, even when I decided one day to create the "Bad Hair Movement"—a movement raising funds to help women in Nepal to get hair-dressing education to become independent.

But I couldn't help what I felt inside my own skin.

I loved the owners, their brand, and their free spirit, but the salon lifestyle was just not for me anymore. After five years, I had changed and grown, and there was nothing they could have done to keep me in — even money would not have changed the fact that I needed something else.

Just thinking about how I would tell them broke my heart as, in a way, I knew it would break our relationship.

At the salon, I was down and became difficult to work with. Then one night, just before Halloween, one of my bosses took me to a fancy sushi place in central London.

We started talking about random kinds of stuff for five min-utes, then suddenly she said: "I can see you are not well at the moment; this is why we are here, what is going on? What can I do to help?"

I stared at her, panicking that the right words would not come out of my mouth. I wanted to throw up. Again, she tried to help, which made me feel so overwhelmed! Then, finally, I found the courage to say: "I cannot do this anymore, after Christmas I will go on holiday, and I won't come back."

Quitting a job is such a hard decision to make. You need to make sure you are resigning for the right reason.

Once I said it out loud to her, my whole body was relieved. After a big cry for both of us, we talked, and today we are friends, and my love and respect for my ex-bosses is beyond what I imagined. Also, I am still working with them but as a freelance social media strategist and recruiter.

Quitting a job is tricky; you feel you are breaking a bond with clients, colleagues, and people you love, but it does not mean that you won't have any relationship at all; the way you decide to leave is all about communication.

Be open, do it with integrity, do it decently. Just be honest and remember that this place welcomed you to be part of their team. Empathy is key!

If you are working in a toxic environment, feel unvalued, bullied, work under the leadership of a narcissistic boss or manager, or even worse; you better leave this place even if you don't want to start a freelance business! But again, quit your job the honourable way; this is also what it means to be professional; you are accountable for your behaviour and decisions no matter what.

When we cannot find our ideal, we need to create it ourselves! This is how so many successful businesses were born; this is how my small businesses were born.

I am sure you can guess what happened next . . . I did it! I set myself up as a freelance hairdresser.

I was not very confident about what my new journey would look like.

But today, I must tell you: I—have—NO—regrets!

Main Pros and cons as a freelancer

Pros	Cons
Choose your clients	Taxes: You need to manage your money wisely
Control of workload	No benefits: you are rarely eligible
Flexibility: hours and locations	Ultimate responsibility for every single task: invoices, stocks, expenses . . .
Independence	Isolation: depending on your location choices
Exposure: more opportunities	No paid time off or maternity/paternity leave
Unlimited earning potential	Unregular workflow
Running every business aspect	Admin tasks
Build your skills	Less job security
Creativity flow	Lack of direction: Nobody to push you but you
Satisfaction improvement	

Freedom cannot be bestowed – it must be achieved.

_____

– *Elbert Hubbard*
(American writer, publisher, and artist)

FAQs

ARE YOU ALONE?

Theoretically, yes, in a way you are alone. However, it's up to you how exactly you set up your business and decide to connect with others or not. Running your own business does not mean that you are going to live a professional life of solitude and loneliness.

If you choose to work from home or mobile (from clients' homes), then yes, professionally, you will be alone.

If you choose to rent a chair/room in a salon, you will probably be less lonely due to the other experts surrounding you in the business.

If you choose to rent your own studio, you can decide whether or not you want somebody else working with you.

If you choose to work from co-working spaces or on set with other people like you, you will probably be surrounded by like-minded freelancers, facing the same issues, and sharing the same journey. Do not underestimate the HBI community; it's like being part of a big family.

To summarise: You will be alone if you decide to be. It's up to you. Do what feels right for you!

Do you have to work crazy hours to earn a decent income?

Again, you are your own boss. This is all about you and your goals! How much do you need to earn? How much do you want to make? Is your price list set up according to your goals?

For example, if you roughly charge £60/hour and your target is to earn £4,000, you will work fewer hours than somebody charging £40/hour.

The critical point is to not mix up turnover and net profit and always remember to save for taxes.

If you manage your stuff right, you will not only survive but thrive!

Sick days and vacations?

As a freelancer, you do not benefit from paid holidays or leave, which means you are not paid if you do not work. So, if you are going on maternity leave, then make sure you saved for it. This is why managing your money well is critical.

How do you get clients?

No client means no money! Sounds scary, but what makes any business is a clientele, and what will make your dream business is a clientele made up of your ideal clients.

How to get clients also depends on where you are working from. Will you be working from a salon? If yes, you will definitely have easier access to more clients. If not, then you'll need a clientele base to start with. Also, some places have walk-in clients, but remember that it increases your chances of competing with other freelancers, so work is not guaranteed.

If you do not have a clientele, it does not mean that you won't be able to establish yourself; however, you will need to work out a solid marketing strategy to promote yourself.

When you are working for a salon and decide to leave, you will automatically have clients who will follow you, and most of the time, you'll be surprised to realise how much they love you! If clients love you, they will be ready to follow you wherever you go.

Here is a big taboo and stressing point when leaving a place: most of the time, the business owner will tell you that the clientele belongs to the salon. Meaning, if you read in between the lines: do not steal my clients!

Fair enough.

A client following a professional leaving a salon: it is just so common. Why? Because we create relationships with our clients, and when your clientele is loyal, you provide more than just a service. In our industry, we get very close to our clients. We sometimes become part of their lives, and they don't want to lose you—the emotion goes beyond money!

It feels that clients do not belong to anybody; they are humans able to make decisions. However, it is your responsibility not to encourage and not push your clients to leave the salon by for example criticising your colleagues or the workplace.

If your clients want to follow you, nobody has to push them; it will just happen, and they'll find you wherever you are. Remember that positive and honest behaviour will always look good to people; when you leave a salon, you can always recommend your colleagues and leave the choice in the hands of your clients.

Whatever is your plan B, always read your employment contract as restrictive covenants, and non-compete clauses (sometimes known as post-termination restrictions) could stop you from establishing your business the way you wanted.

Contract clause aside, do not underestimate how much your clients love you. Stay committed to your work. Have patience and keep working hard.

If you come up with a strong marketing strategy, it will help you build a clientele faster, however, it is highly recommended that you start with a small clientele base. And do not forget that our attitude towards our customers determines their attitude towards us. So be professional, take great care of them, love, and respect them, and they will give it back to you x200!

Part 5

MAKING THE DECISION: GIVE YOURSELF A REALITY CHECK!

BE HONEST WITH yourself, accept your weaknesses and flaws; you may already know what some of these are.

You know what you are capable of and what you aren't (yet) capable of.

SKILLS CHECK

Are you good at the service you want to offer?

Are you able to provide a quality service?

What do you do? Do you specialise in something particular?

How do you make the difference?

Would people pay for what you have to offer?

These are the questions you must ask yourself.

As much as independence can be attractive, you need to be perfectly trained and confident, capable of facing any challenge and fixing any issue during the service.

CONFIDENCE CHECK

Are you confident enough? Confidence is essential - even if sometimes you must fake it! Clients feel comfortable when around self-confident professionals. They need to trust you. They assume, because of your self-assuredness, that the level of your work will be high quality.

Confidence attracts people. It is all about perceptions that are usually based on body language and outward appearances.

An outward projection of confidence can take you a long way, even if you're just starting out your business or if you are not the best in your field.

Fake it till you make it!

MINDSET CHECK

Are you a hard worker? Are you willing to do what it takes to succeed and reach your goals?

Will you be able to sacrifice some drinks with friends over late nights at work? Or some family time over admin paperwork? Will you spend the time needed to work at attracting the right clientele? Are you willing to learn all the new tasks necessary to manage your business?

Also, success is the result of consistency, and consistency is hard work! As a freelancer, you will have many good days, but that doesn't mean bad days won't happen every now and then. When you benefit from so much freedom, everything feels more intense; you can have these super ups and those super downs. However, neglecting any part of your business won't be allowed in downtimes, and the service will always need to remain spot-on.

Remember that something new always requires relearning and adjusting. Once you've got it, though, things become much smoother.

The thing is you need to want it. Passionately.

PAPERWORK CHECK

Are you willing to learn the admin side? Paperwork is not the most pleasant task! If you feel reluctant to start your own business because of the paperwork, I must reassure you, nobody was born with admin skills.

It is all about being serious, consistent, and surrounding your-self with the right professionals and advisors.

Practical digital tools are game-changers. Once you set a rou-tine and a good guide map, it becomes natural. You will also appreciate having full control and managing every side of your business. It is rewarding, and you might end up loving it too!

NEW LOCATION CHECK

Do you know where you will work from?

The location(s) where you want to set yourself up is an important point; this is where you will be seeing your clien-tele. When you announce that you are changing location, we always assume that you are changing for the better, and your clientele will automatically have high expectations.

The location is critical as it will set your standards, while its cost will set the tone of your brand and price rates.

CLIENTELE CHECK

Do you have a clientele base? This is a significant point to investigate.

Without clients, you won't make money. Depending on where you are planning to work from, relying on walk-ins might be insufficient. If you plan to work from home, offer mobile services, or work from private spaces, you might not be able to get walk-ins.

Consider if you already have a clientele base that will support you in your new project. For example, if you need to move to another area or another city, will they follow you?

Try also to work out who your clientele archetypes are:

Who is your ideal client? Who are your current clients? What do they have in common? What type of business would attract them? Who are your most loyal clients? Are you ready to work on a strategy to build up your dream clientele?

SURVIVAL CHECK

Do you know how much you need to earn to survive?

You do not want to run a business just for the sake of it! Neither do you just want to survive; you want to live, right?

The chance to set your own salary sounds like a dream. But freelancers know the reality is a little more complicated. In the beginning, you might not make a considerable profit, but it does not mean that you won't get paid.

How much income do you need to live, including some extra for unpredictable expenses? Here is a list of things you might want to include:

- Mortgage
- Rent

- Council tax
- Gas, electricity, water rates
- Insurances
- Food
- Clothing
- Telephone
- Entertainment (meals, drinks, cinema)
- Subscriptions (gym, magazines, etc.)
- Car tax and insurance
- Vehicle service and maintenance
- Children's expenditure and presents
- Savings plan
- Hire charges (TV, video, etc.)
- Credit card
- Personal loan repayments
- Family events

I would like to bring your attention to one point: I am talking about survival, assessing how much money you will need to survive, and determining your minimum necessary income.

The amount you need to survive is a significant number to consider, as there's no point in being stressed out with your company's financial and emotional problems plus survival.

Later, the question will be: will the business plan you made allow you to live or survive? Especially at the beginning, when you start with a small budget, every single penny counts; the more money you are saving, the more secure you will feel.

When I made my business plan, I made sure the monthly money I needed would be achievable from the first month. When I started working, I noticed that I made money straight away. I could have taken more money home, but because I wanted to build a positive cash flow and invest in growing my new business, I decided to give myself the minimum I needed to survive as a wage.

To be honest, I am glad I decided to manage my business that way; when the 2020 UK lockdown happened, I had no income, and the money I had in the bank really made the difference.

Whatever the amount you need to survive, make sure it will be achievable from the first month - or make sure you have a plan B!

It is your business, your money, your choices.

FUNDS CHECK

What financial resources do you have to start your own business? Yes, we are talking pounds, dollars, euros, whatever the currency is: we are talking about money.

It is interesting to financially evaluate how much you can invest in your business. If you don't have a lot of money, it doesn't mean that you won't be able to start your business, but a serious check is necessary.

You might wonder if starting your own business is expensive? It can be, but the secret has always been you have to spend money to make money! It's hard to make money in a business without investing some money in supplies, products, advertisements, or other business expenses. When creating a business, entrepreneurs are often looking for ways to cut costs. They fear losing money if anything goes wrong. That's understandable. Once my business advisor told me that the money you are willing to invest shows how much you believe in your project. After all, money is the lifeblood of any business, and once you run out of it, it's over.

Also, sometimes spending money saves you money.
I got a £300 hairdryer that is faster than my old £90 one. I work in a co-working space, and I pay for my salon styling chair per hour; this investment saves me time - and therefore money! Of course, when things are tight with money, it can be tricky . . . but if I had to choose, I would rather save money by buying less than buying cheap. What about you?
Investment knowledge is essential for any single business; a lot of parameters are to be considered.

Your main expenses will probably include:

- The fees relating to your company registration if an accountant does it for you.
- The purchase of the small materials and potential tools.
- The purchase of the consumables: some suppliers require a bulk stock order.
- Marketing expenses: website, business cards, etc.
- Extra fees . . . such as a card machine if you want to offer this payment method.

I will now share with you my main expenses when I started my own freelance business as a hairstylist and colour expert. I have hesitated for a long time whether to share this or not. But in the end, this book is about sharing, isn't it?

Your attention please!

This is not the right or best way, neither what you need to do or spend to set up your own freelance company. It is all about personal choices and funds available to you but also the money you are willing to pay. I built my business based on my budget, the money I was ready to invest in, considering the professional advice I received—please note, professional advice is definitely recommended at this stage. I have documented my business start-up costs to give you some insight into "typical" costs. What I want is to provide you with a head start for your own research and I hope that you will be able to get set up quickly.

Expense	Description	Total
Accountant	Company registration	£70
Tools	I bought bare essentials such as combs, clips, and brushes. I did not have everything previously. I compared prices and did not buy anything fancy, just the minimum necessary to reduce my initial investment cost but still allow me to work comfortably.	£300
Consumables / stock	I decided to invest in an extensive stock as my distributor had special offers available. Also, I got a lot of free materials such as aprons, bowls, and tools. I saved money as it was things that I really needed.	£2295
Marketing	I decided to create a logo myself to start with. I also made my website using a German website builder and an all-in-one hosting solution. I designed and printed business cards online.	£150
	I hired a photographer to help me build some clean and on-brand content for my social media.	£400
Extra fees	Card machine, stationery, software purchase.	£200
Other	I added money to my business bank account to start off my business, paid a law professional to draft my T&C and bought insurance.	£1500

NET total spent: £4,915

My accountant registered my company and advised me on the correct company status. I hired her for 1 year, which did cost me £80/month. I purchased a lot of tools I didn't have—but the essentials only. A couple of months later, my small business was doing well, so I decided that I was able to buy a fancy hairdryer.

I also invested in an extensive stock to benefit from an offer. I knew that my clientele would buy retail products from me, so I also bought a little stock to start me off—retail has helped me make profits and, during the lockdown, it has been a very nice income while I could not work.

To spend less money first, I could have bought a smaller stock and ordered the products I needed weekly. However, it is again a personal choice. The tricky part has been to store everything - but money-wise, it was totally worth it!

I decided to work with only one brand because I love their products, and their ethos is in line with my brand. However, as a freelancer, you don't have to work with one brand only; you can pick all your favourite products in different brands, which is another freedom that really makes the difference.

As a freelancer, it used to be almost impossible to set up an account with brands. However, mentalities are now evolving, and the most notable brands now see freelancers as proper businesses. What a fantastic victory!

When you do not know what you want, you are more likely to remain unsatisfied; this is the main reason why I did not hire a brand stylist and website designer. Going through burnout, I was psychologically not in the best place to decide what I wanted or not, and it felt like a waste of money and time. So, I used a platform and did the job myself. Today, I now fancy a good-looking brand with a stronger identity. I finally have time and headspace to think about what I want; I have grown, and I am in the process of rebranding.

You will notice that I did not spend money on advertising myself on any paid platform. This is because I had a small client base, but this client base was totally my dream clients. Luckily, some mobile cutting experts were sending me their clients for colour as we had a similar clientele which helped a lot in the beginning. So instead of attracting new clients from the crowd, I decided to create a referral system. My ideal clients were more likely to have similar people around them, so I decided to bet on word of mouth, which rewarded my loyal clients. After seeing me five times, a client becomes a platinum client and is entitled to 2 secret cards a year (referral cards). So, they and whoever they refer both benefit from a bespoke hair treatment. As a result, I have grown my clientele by 35% in the first year.

If I look back, what I would change is my choice of photographer. I would choose somebody with a portfolio closer to what I was looking for and someone able to shoot hair pics - even if I had to pay more. My first photoshoot provided me with professional content for a whole year, and my website got incredible pictures that represented my brand well.

I know many people who started with less than half of what I invested, and they've smashed it too. When building a business, we do not have the same strategy, needs, and budget—it is all about calculations . . .

The freelancing community is growing fast in the HBI, causing even a staff shortage in the most significant cities; some business consultants of the HBI now offer packages to help you start your freelance business... It obviously comes with a price, but why not if your budget allows you this luxury!

When starting your freelance business, do what feels the best for you, surround yourself with experts, and think about your own strategy.

Freelancer by April.C

Part 6

WHAT IS A BUSINESS PLAN?

A BUSINESS PLAN introduces your business; it tells a beautiful story about its future, presenting your objectives and means. Finally, it will outline all the details of your company.

A good plan should answer this question: why will *your* business succeed when so many others fail?

This business plan is going to help you understand if starting your own business is a good idea.

IS IT COMPULSORY TO DRAW UP A BUSINESS PLAN?

A business plan is a document that will help you to clarify your ideas; it will give you direction, help you as you grow, and be used as an official document if you need funding to start your business.

Drawing up a business plan can be a tedious exercise— it's the first step to understanding the potential of your project, your strategy and clarifying where it is leading you in terms of timescale. But ultimately, it will help you decide whether it is a good idea and help you determine if you will take the leap or not—Are you going to establish yourself as a freelancer and become your own boss?

It is not the most straightforward task, and you can find help by using a consultant/freelancer specialised in this topic.

A business plan is a plan set at a specific point in time. It will never be 100% correct, but it should let people see how risky and realistic your idea is. Even if we usually start working on a business plan to show to others (banks, investors), in the end, the primary user who will benefit from the business plan is the creator themselves — aka you!

A business plan is not compulsory, but you have no reason not to do it!

A classic business plan skeleton would look like this:

Executive summary

A summary that you can use to briefly
describe your project. This should be done
at the end once you complete your plan.

Company description

What do you do? History/key dates
Who are you? Background? Motivation?
What service do you want to provide?

Who is your customer?

Who do you target?

Demographic?

Location?

Profession?

Competition?

What is your mission?

Vision?

Brand?

Values?

Services?

Costs?

What problem do you solve?

Marketing plan

Where are your clients?

How do you read your clients?

How will you promote yourself?

Financial plan

Funding

Cash flow analysis

Profit/loss analysis

Details of your turnover drivers

Funding

You may not have the necessary funds, but this doesn't mean you won't be able to go ahead with your project— outsourcing funds is an option.

---

4 TRUSTED FUNDING METHODS

Family, friends, contacts
It's common for parents or friends to financially support you in the early stages of your business. Make a list of your contacts, try to find out who would believe in your project, and trust you enough to lend you money to achieve your dream.

Bank loans
A common way to fund your business is a bank loan. If you do not have any background, you will need a solid and credible business plan. Also, make sure you do some research about the different types of loans and interest rates.

Crowdfunding
Raising money online from the public is becoming very popular. However, keep in mind that it can take longer to reach your target!

Business angels

Angel investors are wealthy individuals who provide funding in exchange for a share of your business.

Borrowing money can put extra pressure on your shoulders. Remember that mixing money and friends or relatives can have an impact on your relationship. It is essential to consider all the options and ask the help of a professional such as a business plan consultant, business advisor, or accountant if you feel you need to—you do not have to do this alone!

It is also good to check if the Government offers any small business grants or start-up loans.

If you finance your project yourself or with a bank, you will still be your business's owner, boss, and decision-maker. However, if you use family members or even business angels, it means you may have people entering your "capital." They may become shareholders; in other words, they may also own your company which can be positive or negative, but you need to acknowledge that you will not always be ultimately free to do what you want.

Make sure you do a lot of research and build up a concrete plan.

Will a business plan make your small business a guaranteed success? No, but it will help you succeed, determining if being a freelancer could work for you right now.

Part 7

TAKING THE LEAP

PROCESS GUIDE

WHAT HAPPENS ONCE you've made the decision?
I can't stress these points enough: surround yourself with the right people/professionals! Never be afraid to ask questions and connect!

To sum up, you have been working toward freelancing and starting your very own business in the hair and beauty world. You took this very seriously; you did a lot of research and spent time considering all the details.

The reality may be that after drawing up your business plan, the outcome came up with a result that was not encouraging enough to take the leap, and it could push you to take a step back. It can be very heart-breaking —I know—but WELL DONE to you if you choose to make this tough decision! It takes a lot to work on a project and admit that it might not be a suitable or the correct time for you at this very moment. This might be disappointing, but it is crucial to understand why.

Do not give up; keep working toward your dreams, and they will come true. Take time to reflect on why you have been tempted to start your own business. Is it because you are unhappy with where you're at? Is it perhaps the right time to think about a plan B?

Doing this research will never be a waste of time; it teaches you a lot, and it will give you the confidence to do it again when the perfect opportunity will show up.

BUT—what about if you are ready?

On the other hand, once you have done a serious self-check, thought about it more than twice, drawn up a valid business plan, and finally decided to take the leap: WELL DONE! Of course, there's a lot of work left to do, but no worries, I will get you started!

MINDSET

There is nothing more creative than a healthy mind in a healthy body. When creating a business, you genuinely need to be connected with yourself. Working toward your dream requires your full energy and attention.

Look after yourself, make sure you feel balanced, feed your soul and your body and let's embrace this new project.

From now on, write down anything that will help you to build yourself and your plan.

10 TIPS FOR WORKING EFFECTIVELY ON YOUR EXCITING PROJECT

We all have goals, but do we always do everything to achieve them?

I want to climb Everest; for years, I can keep talking about my ambition to anybody happy to listen that soon I will do it. But, if I don't do anything for it to happen, will I ever climb Everest? Certainly not, which will certainly affect my credibility on the way.

But if I decide to book some time off work, train, buy my tickets, and organise my trip, does it sound like a significant move toward my goal?

Do you think I am going to climb Everest?

Well, stuff happens, but I am more likely to succeed!

Can you see the big picture?

The secret to achieving a project is to schedule and perform on a deadline; time management will be a game-changer. Life is busy; we tend to start so many things that we never achieve, like learning a new sport or clearing up our wardrobe; we often run out of time because we don't prioritise these things. So now, it's about dedicating yourself to yourself, giving yourself and your future a chance to succeed; it's time to schedule yourself to work on your business, plan, and smash it!

Tip 1 – Suitable work environment

Choose the spot where you will be working on your new business wisely. Work from a location where you feel inspired, relaxed, focused, and not distracted.
I like working from the hub of my gym; I drink my favourite protein smoothie and listen to music on my headphones. This is where I feel calm and productive.
How and where are you the most focused?

Tip 2 – Energy peak hours

Make sure to identify at what time you are the most productive. For example, I am an early bird; I wake up at 5am and I am the most energised and creative between 6am and 12pm.

If you are a night owl, you might process differently.

When do you feel the most productive?

Tip 3 – Run a routine

Make sure you develop a consistent and repeatable process that will help you to be more effective.

A routine is made of small details. For example, before going to bed, I make sure my to-do list is ready for the following day; I also make sure I have at least one thing planned that excites me as it motivates me to wake up and get on with my day.

You need to find a routine that sets you up as soon as you wake up; I need meditation, skincare, some exercise, and breakfast in the morning, then I can start working. I know myself, I could spend hours working without even self-checking, which is not ideal; therefore I set up a timer every 2 hours to remind me to check if I need a drink, stretch, stand up, or need a few minutes of break.

What is your routine going to be like?

Tip 4 – Prep a plan

Draw up a plan, set a schedule, and give yourself deadlines. Do not multitask - creating requires deep thinking, and multitasking is less suitable. Instead, be organised enough to eliminate stress.

Working on this kind of project can be overwhelming as your brain will keep going through things all day and night. Writing down a plan and setting a deadline will give your brain a break as you will send it a signal: "I've got it! It's all under control." And you will feel less stressed and way more productive.

What is your plan?

Tip 5 – Avoid distractions

When you are productive and inspired, distractions can slow you down. Turn off your phone notifications and all social media if necessary. Let people around know that you need to work and do not want to be disturbed. Focus your mind on *What's Good for Your Business.*

What could be distracting you?

Tip 6 – Take a break

Even if you don't think or feel you need it, take a break; your brain and body do. Go for a walk, breathe in some fresh air. You can exercise as well; it is one of the most excellent productivity tools in the world.

Taking a break when focusing on a project always feels to be the worst to me. It's like I am wasting my precious time. But, in the end, it's not wasting time; it allows your body to relax and your brain to function better, resulting in working more effectively.

What does the best break look like to you?

Tips 7 – Connect well

Do not overload your brain with unnecessary information. Your brain will be busy enough with your plan, and you want to feed it with interesting information such as podcasts, books, articles, and videos relating to your new project.

Join groups, forum communities, or ask people to tell you about their own experiences—it's so valuable!

When I work on something big, I always talk about my project to two trusted people. It can sound weird but expressing your thoughts out loud and brainstorming with somebody else can be so helpful!

I choose my people carefully. I am not going to ask advice from like-minded people, but individuals that are different than me, the ones who will probably challenge me on my ideas. Where there is discomfort, there is growth. It's not always the easiest to accept criticism, but this is what you are after at this stage. What you need is trustable, different, and honest people.

With whom are you going to connect?

Tip 8 – Well-being first!

Do the little things that make you happy and help you to relax. Working on high-importance projects can be stressful, and as stress is counterproductive, it is crucial to take care of yourself more than ever.

Do not overwork and avoid working at night – and keeping away from screens at night is a must!

In general, do not neglect your food and nutrients. When working, if you like snacking, select your fuel carefully to avoid sugar spikes as they will slow down your productivity. What nourishes your soul and contributes to your well-being?

Tip 9 – Get lost, please!

Do not be available to everybody. You are building up the new step of your life, and you are busy enough. Some people you love—or not—can suck your energy away. You will definitely look after them if you want to, but later on.

We all know the importance of choosing the people surrounding us. Good partners or friends will stand by you and accept that you are working on achieving something, and it means that you won't always make the time for them when it's busy. It could mean that they will go out without you, your partner or flat mates will potentially have to handle more housework. Of course, our loved ones should always be what's matter the most, but when the time comes for you to build your future, they mustn't make you feel bad but support you and your dream.

Be clear on your relationships and communicate what you need from people as they will not always figure out what you are going through.

Right now, keep sending that beautiful energy to yourself!

Tip 10 – Be unapologetically YOU!

Work toward your dream without worrying about decisions that could upset other people. Some people are unable to look at other people grow. It is okay. You are not responsible for their happiness, just yours.

This is how it starts; set your mindset and be determined to create this incredible business and the perfect setup for yourself!

The unhappiest people in this world are those who care the most about what other people think.
_____

– *C. JoyBell C*

Part 8

THE FREELANCER STARTER CHECKLIST

THE FREELANCER STARTER Checklist is the ultimate checklist to start you off! A business creation process can be overwhelming because if you are a newbie, it can be hard to think about all the details involved—you don't want to miss out on something that could have made the difference!

Online, you will find many different pieces of info for freelancers, but they are not always related to the HBI and can be misleading.

The Freelancer Starter Checklist won't do the work on your behalf, but it will help you brainstorm, guide you, and show you the direction—it's full of tips and tricks. It will show you the way through the essential steps of your project. Remember, there is no obligation and, wherever you are in the world, do not forget to double-check what is compulsory or not in your country.

Going through the *Freelancer Starter Checklist*, you will understand what needs to be done, and this guidance will boost your confidence. Make sure to manage your project effectively but do not forget to make the process easy and fun; working on the next step of your career is really exciting!

After each topic, you will find some pages designed for your own notes; use them to record all your ideas as you read and use them again to brainstorm later.
After reading this, you will finally know where to start!

Are you ready?

BUILDING A BRAND

Building a brand is what you need to do first. As a freelancer, your brand will be ALL about yourself; YOU are representing your business. Remember that people love you for who you are.

Let me get straight to the point: show off your identity, be authentic, and your brand will speak for you. If you build a brand around something that just sells—for now—and if it doesn't reflect your personality, it won't look legit, and you might not be able to sustain it in the long run.

Visually, a brand is complex. It is a unique combination of the right colours, fonts, patterns, designs, and much more that will connect others with what you do and help you make the right impression. In addition, your brand's style will stimulate emotions: you will establish an emotional connection between your clients and your business.

Every single element is essential. Do not underestimate the power of colours and what they communicate to our brain. Your brand will make you recognisable and set a professional look showing a consistent message on all platforms.

At this stage, you need to consider whether you want to work with a professional brand designer.

A professional brand designer or a brand identity consultant will guide you through the process of creating your brand and distinctive brand authenticity. First, make sure you choose somebody who sounds interested in your project and who you are excited to work with. Then, like in the case of a photographer, choose the one with a portfolio that is not just beautiful but also speaks and resonates with you. When working with creatives, always make sure their work and style reflect what you need.

Alternatively, you might consider the less expensive option and work out that brand on your own; this is totally cool too. First, however, make sure you are doing a lot of research so you can produce quality logos and designs that you can share on your social media and print on documents such as business cards. Cheap does not look good!

Whatever option you choose, you will have to work out your brand's essence, aspirations, and intention.

My best advice would be to create a mood board to visualise the skeleton of your brand better. Also, if you decide to work with a brand stylist or designer, it will serve as support to share your vision.

When I created my first freelance company, I had no idea of what a brand was. So, I just went online, chose a logo, added my name, and made business cards and flyers. This brand was nothing exciting or personal; my brand would have never stood out between 10 business cards left on a countertop. Apparent lack of knowledge, I know; another lesson learnt.

I like to be crafty when creating a mood board as it inspires me more than my virtual board on Pinterest. I stick all my ideas on a wall that I can see every day at home. I add pictures, colours, notes with inspirations, print photos, images cut out from magazines—anything that would inspire me to grow this idea. I also carry a notebook wherein I write down any idea that comes to my mind.

The best thing is to get it right first time. However, you can always rebrand later, keeping the main essence without changing it all.

Once your brand is on point, all your content will be spread around your website and social media. It will be much easier to build all your platforms as the only line to follow will be the essence of your brand. Make sure you love your business image; it will be easier to market and sell if you are proud of it.

Some questions to ask yourself when starting off your mood board:

- What is your brand story?
- What are your values?
- Why are you doing what you do?
- What is the core of what you do?
- Where do you position yourself compared to other businesses?
- What makes your brand unique?
- What is your mission?
- What is your story?
- How do you stand out from the crowd?
- What colours inspire you?
- What images inspire you?
- What brands inspire you?

This brand creation process can be very fun and will definitely make things more real: This-is-REALLY-happening!

Notes about Building a brand.

FREELANCER

CREATE A WEBSITE

A website is not compulsory but highly recommended. A professional-looking website will make you look more legitimate and set you apart from the general freelancer crowd. People who don't know you will be able to visualise and understand your image and business. You will be able to showcase your work and your vibe.

Since day one, I have had my website, and it has been helpful to show off my new brand to my current clients. I kept it simple; I added important information such as my co-working salon location details, brand value, business terms and conditions, and more. Although the booking page is the most visited, I added a handy "booking" button to encourage bookings at any time of the day or night. You can use your website to display your services and price list.

When I have a new client, they can discover my brand and who I am. People get the info they need, and they rarely question me, which is time-saving when you work on your own. Let people understand your standards.

Why not consider adding a blog to help with your website visibility? Blogging can show off your expertise and drive traffic to your website.

Did you know that a blog can be monetised and generate income? You may like the idea, but you may not feel you can actually write a blog post, and this is okay. The option could be to hire freelance blog writers; you will only need to provide them with the content and your ideas. They will do the job for you, ensuring it's SEO optimised (search engine optimisation). Managing a blog can be quite a lot of work, but money or anything in life does not come for free.

You will need to build up the content of your website and work on your brand before anything to make sure everything goes together. Building your business, you'll tend to reduce the length of your to-do list unconsciously. For example, while creating your website, you might wonder if buying a domain is necessary. To me, any business with an online presence should own a domain for multiple reasons, but mainly to protect copyrights and drive and increase traffic as much as possible.

Buying a domain is cheap and looks professional; you have no reason not to do it. However, you are free to do it or not.

Here is a list of what you may want your website to display:

- Logo
- Catchphrase
- Your profile
- Your work ethic / core values

- Services
- Price list
- Terms and conditions of business
- Your location
- Contact details
- Online booking option (button, link)
- Social media link
- Newsletter (box pop-up, link)

You can decide to do this alone and create your website through a website builder such as Wix or Squarespace. It is easy, fast, cost-effective, and you can create a beautiful and professional-looking website with some creativity.

You could also decide to work alongside a professional web designer. When choosing a web designer, do not hesitate to request a lot of quotes from companies. The prices will range from reasonable to double what your budget is, and you want to make sure that you are paying a fair price for an appropriate service.

As the beauty industry is based on the visual, make sure to include beautiful imagery.
Professional and high-resolution shots are highly recommended, and a good photographer will be game-changing.

An image will create an emotion in a few seconds in a way that text can't do. In just a second you can convince a client that you are the one! That's why it is essential to make sure your imagery is accurate, on-brand, and reflects your work. If you want to up your game, you could include a video of your work and create the proper experience feel through your website.

When hiring a web designer, my number one tip is to make sure you can edit your website independently, without constantly asking the designer to do the job for you and adding payment for their time.

Also, you must consider that growing your business will also mean growing as a person; at some point, you will probably have to refresh your website.

Your website content should be on-brand and flow naturally. However, what I call the "compulsory about me page" can be tricky. The most challenging bit has been to work out my profile; I felt very vulnerable and shy to talk about myself and my experiences. Working on your own is different from working for a company; as one person behind all the work, *you* are the brand.

The purpose of a profile is to introduce yourself, make known your skills and unique way of doing things. Therefore, it would be best if you looked trustworthy and professional to attract your ideal clients.

The challenge is to do it without up-selling yourself too much (you don't want to look egocentric!) Also, do not forget the essential portrait photo; people want to see you—make sure that your attitude will represent you and your brand.

When working on any project, I use freelancers regularly. I like to e-meet and work alongside passionate creatives. I usually hire them on apps such as Upwork, Fiverr, or equivalent freelancer platforms to assist me with many different things. For example, I hire them to create promo videos or websites, proofread official documents or design illustrations for my newsletters. It's so exciting to work with entrepreneurs worldwide.

My graphic designer lives in America. I checked out her profile and website to ensure she was trustworthy then decided to work with her. This is how convincing and valuable a website can be—if you take it seriously, your clients will, too!

Notes about creating a website

PART 8

LOCATION

The location of your new business will not only set the tone of your brand but will also directly impact your price list.

As a freelancer of the HBI, you will benefit from all the flexibility you always wanted; this is your opportunity to set yourself up at home and welcome your clients there or work mobile, traveling to their homes. You can also choose to rent a chair within a salon or a co-working salon/space - you could even create a salon in a van and drive away if you wanted.

As a freelancer, you can choose to work from a few different locations and enjoy a life of absolute freedom!

I decided to establish myself in one of the first UK's co-working space for hair and beauty freelancers located in central London.

If you wonder what a co-working salon is, I will define it as a co-working space for hair and beauty experts. They all function differently; they have their own concept, rules, charging system, pros, and cons.

I believe that co-working salons can benefit any hair and beauty expert in multiple ways. For example, when I decided to quit my salon to work for myself, I could not get my head

126

around looking for a space, signing a lease, and the hassle of the costs, paperwork, and bills. I had never thought about a co-working salon, but when I found it, it was my Holy Grail; I understood right away that this concept meant that I could run my own business from a stunning place without lease commitments or risks.

In my co-working salon, I rent my chair per hour, pay a flat monthly fee, and benefit from high-standard services that add value to the experience I provide to my clients - and I charge for it.

When selecting your co-working space, you need to understand how this space will help and support your business daily. For example:

- Can you store your tools there?
- Do you get assistance with bookings?
- Who's welcoming your clients?
- Is it open every day?
- Can you work before and after opening hours?
- Can you use any brand?
- Can you cancel or freeze your membership anytime?
- Is there any material provided?
- Do they provide refreshments for you and your clients?
- Is there any hub to socialise and organise business meetings?

In co-working spaces, what I love, and what all freelancers need, is to connect and socialise with like-minded people. In the end, there isn't any competition; you are just professionals sharing the same love for what you do under the same roof.

To work from the co-working salon I have chosen, I had to set my prices higher than what my clients used to pay.

I must admit that I knew my clientele would have to commute at least 2 hours back and forth to see me, which was adding to their expenses. I was unsure whether my current clients would travel to me. It was scary to contemplate. However, I was very motivated to build a clientele, and I knew I would provide the dream experience I always wanted. So, with determination, I stuck to my standards, the best or nothing, and I went for it. In the end, my clients love it, they pay more, but they also get more.

 Know your standards and values and believe in you; you know best!

A new location can be game changer for your business, but wherever you decide to work, make sure you can afford it.

Example: *If you are tattooing eyebrows for £40/h but the room you hire costs you £35/hours, you will hardly make any money!*

You also need to make sure that the place chosen reflects the essence of your brand. For example, you are a talented beauty professional with incredible skills and a beautiful website that sells high-end services but work from a cheap-looking place in a dodgy area; if not disappointing, it will be misleading for your clients.

When considering a new location, assessing the type of salon your client was loyal to in the past can be very helpful.
If you decide to relocate your business far away from your previous location, you need to know if your clients will follow you or not: your clientele base is everything!

Today I can tell you that I am genuinely impressed by how many people followed to support me - and so will you be too.

As a hair or beauty expert, this type of client will make you feel highly valued, and, suddenly, all the hard work you had to put in is worth it.

Wherever you will be working from, it will need to be your vibe. Make sure to feel comfortable, as your emotions will dramatically impact the experience you are providing. I like to set up my station with business cards, candles, treats, and plants; it is a recognisable atmosphere I create for my guest and myself. Sometimes it is very stressful to choose a location when you don't know your clients' preferences; often, the easiest way to find out is simply to ask—a poll on Instagram, e-mailing, or just asking the question directly.

TIP! Only choose what works best for you and your clientele. If you decide to up your game and work from multiple places, do not forget to consider the commuting fees involved. Whether or not you need material—think about how you will carry it and where you will stock all your things.

Notes about choosing a location

FREELANCER

Pricing — services

When setting up your business, you'll need to create a list of services that you'd like to offer. For instance: I don't like doing perms, so it is not on my list of services. It is *your* business! It is imperative to do what you like and what feels the most appropriate. If you are a beautician but if you do not want to wax bikinis, just don't do it! This is your prerogative.

How do you package your skills and expertise and offer them to a customer?

When you are an experienced professional, a list of services is relatively easy to build up. But what about your price list? Pricing is such a sensitive topic, and so many factors need to be considered. The cost of a service is all about numbers; it's a calculation, but how to assess the added value of this service, and how much do you charge for your skills and expertise?

Fifteen years ago, when I built my first business, I travelled to clients' homes. To set my prices, I thought: "let's see what other people are charging." Unfortunately, this meant that I was deciding to compete on price instead of value and I ignored that my costs of sale were probably different from those of my competitors. If you wonder what value really means, well, quite frankly, that's what customers believe the service is worth to them.

So, there I went, my young unexperienced self, checked out other nail salons around. I assessed their price lists then decided to reduce my prices. I justified my decision with the knowledge that, as I was not renting a salon, I could be cheaper, and perhaps catch some salon clients who wanted a more private and more affordable service at home.

Setting prices based on competitors' price lists; is a common mistake—it means that you are assuming the competitors have done their research while also having the same costs as you. In fact, you cannot just charge what other competitors charge simply because:

- You might not have the same expenses.
- You might not provide the same services and added value.
- You might not have the same profit goal.

Another common mistake is to copy the prices of the last business you worked in without a proper strategy. We all tend to set our first price list not too far from what our clients used to pay; you don't want to shock your clientele; however, undercharging could lead to your loss.

When discussing undercharging, we don't talk about low pricing—undercharging means charging for less than what it costs you.

Pricing low is not bad, especially if you want to penetrate a market; however, you can't spend more money than you make; otherwise, the profit margin won't be lower than it should be but non-existent.

You could price low to build up a clientele, but it will need to be for a short period only, then you will need to increase your prices afterward, so it becomes profitable.

On the other hand, overcharging could dramatically impact your chances of success. So, when it is about price, always seek balance. Clients always need to see the value, and as a new business, you'll have to make sure your marketing will show it off.

What also dictates the price is the demand:

- Are you an expert?
- Do you offer a unique service?
- Are you currently working on waiting list only?

Let's put ourselves in the shoes of Mr. V!
If Mr. V decides to book a £90 barber, he is not expecting the same service or vibe as if he were booking the £8 bar-

ber because Mr. V will expect a premium and high standard experience.

It's all about the details, a great location, a spot-on brand, and everything that will make him feel unique and privileged.

Mr. V will be expecting to be greeted and treated nicely; he will expect you to be available to him. Mr. V will expect a beautiful and maintained space, an impeccable and enjoyable moment. What Mr. V is buying is not just a good haircut, but a package including the best service. I'm sure you understand, the experience factor is crucial.

Have you ever heard about luxury-level service?

Anything luxury must be charged at a higher price. When thinking about the client's experience, the very best at this game are high-end brands; they are so good at it!

So now, on a smaller scale, how can we imitate luxury brands to add value to the services of our small businesses?

Talking about luxury-level service doesn't mean that your products or services are expensive; it is more about creating the experience for your customer.

Consistent willingness to be professional is crucial. Are you providing high-end customer service, putting extra care and love into what you do? Striving to raise the bar and provide nothing but the best will also massively increase the value of your service in the eye of the customer.

When I was traveling to people's homes, I spent a lot of time driving (adding to expense) and therefore saw fewer clients a day than if I was providing my services in a salon. When you are at clients' homes, it's a one-on-one service. It's a luxury when you think about it - they get your expertise within the comfort of their home. Your clients don't have to plan time to visit you anywhere, arrange the commute, or child-care. Visiting their home, I saved them time and money.

Of course, working from customers' homes meant that I had less control over my environment. Life can be unpredictable, and it was harder to manage the timings, so I tended to work longer. I clearly remember my appointments being disrupted by children or friends popping in for coffee. One client once even let her dinner burn in the oven; we had to finish her nails in the garden as the smoke in the house was unbearable!

If this book had been in my hand at that time, I would have created a solid policy to establish rules, save time and money. But, lucky you, if you keep reading, you will go through all about the importance of terms and conditions of business.

Working at customers' homes is a very private and unique experience. I used to bring sweets and treats; I always made sure to set a lovely table, including a mirror and adding expensive-looking LED candles to create a chilled ambiance. I would turn off my phone, bring slippers and try to be as discreet as possible to respect their home intimacy. I was very available to my clients, and I would often work until 11pm to please them.

Even if the service was spot on and luxury level, could I have charged premium prices?
No, because I was not experienced enough, and I was not an expert at doing nails. Charging a premium price for a service you haven't mastered doesn't feel premium, and it would not have made sense to me or my clients.

Defining how to charge the right amount for your expertise: what a headache!

I remember when I first started to work in London, balayaging hair was not a thing. The salon where I worked built up its reputation on highlights - working in two on one customer's head. They would put hundreds of foils in a record time.
One day someone asked me for help. They needed me to find a way to please a young client who came with an Instagram pic. Free-hand balayage has been the answer. I painted and

blended bleach on her hair, and in 30 min it was done; less than two hours later, the client was out. They decided to charge the price of another service that was 45 min too as I had been "very quick."

If I can do an expensive-looking and spot-on service in 45min, does it mean that I should charge this service for 45 minutes of my time?
When you get better at something, you tend to do it quicker. So, does this mean that you should charge the client less?

In my opinion, the answer is NO, absolutely not!
Moral of the story: Time does not reflect your ability.

In the end, you do not want to charge per hour, but you really want to charge for your expertise, for the time you spent working your butt off to learn all the techniques that make your touch so unique. Making the difference is an investment of time and money - you invested into your education to master your craft, and you need to charge for it - always making sure it will be profitable, of course!

You are not in business for charity. You don't just want to survive; you want to LIVE!

_____

– *April. C*

When setting your prices, you will also need to understand how clients or potential clients perceive the value of your services.

If a higher price means quality in their eyes, low prices could mean fewer bookings and sales as your clients will assume that the value isn't there.

Pricing is one of the most complex but most important things for a business to get right.

Price too low and you will lose money, and if you price too high you may discourage potential customers. This is where the psychology of pricing makes the difference.

Understanding how your customers feel about price and value will guide you through setting the right price for your services.
Your price list should align with the value of your business's service for its customers, bearing in mind your position compared to your competitors.

Wherever you are, there will always be other businesses around. We need to understand why clients choose to wax their eyebrows for £35 instead of going to the next-door shopping centre to get an equivalent result for £8. Same scenario with barbers, why do people choose to spend £90 in a barbershop when they can walk into the shop next door and get a haircut for less than ten quid?

To justify your prices is essential for your customer to understand why they are paying this price. It is safe to say that your price list will naturally select your clientele.

Make your business a cohesive one balancing service, value, and pricing.

Wherever you are, there will always be a client that tells you that the salon down the road charges less for the "same service." Such a frustrating situation where you tend to take this remark personally because what you hear is that you are "too expensive." If you lack self-confidence, you might even hear that you are not "worth your prices."

It used to leave me speechless that people could eventually not get why two businesses were pricing the same service differently.

But the client at this point only looks at things from the point of view of what they are personally paying out; it's nothing against you, your skills, or professionalism.

In this situation, if your price list is in concordance with the service's value, you can always give them the correct answer and justify your prices. Set yourself exactly where you want to be. Some ideas to add value to your service:

- Tailor the client journey
- Add your magic touch
- Enhance existing treatments/services
- Mini treatments/service for time-poor clients
- Add-ons
- Follow up your appointments
- Personalised advice
- Complimentary drinks
- Complimentary massage
- Be accessible and available
- Signature service
- Collect feedback from your customers
- Bespoke products/experience

Be creative: no one is you!

Also, another important note:

Profit is different than turnover. Suppose you get £1,000 a day in the till; not all of it is going into your pocket. You cannot consider this as an income: make a meticulous calculation considering your goals as well.

A good friend of mine worked in a hair salon booked up every day; they were the most expensive salon in the area. I always thought that they were doing very well. However, they never profited because they would never cover their costs and charges even if they were more expensive than the other businesses around.

Wise advice I received from a savvy accountant ten years ago: if you do not charge profit, you won't make any!

Moral: work out that price list; otherwise, you could end up fully booked every day and not make any money at all.

The correct prices will even help you to maximise your profits. Let's break down what you need to consider when setting up a price:

Right price

=

Time invested

Price your time (this includes your education, expertise…)

+

Cost of sales

Direct costs of producing the services

that you sell to your customers.

This amount includes the cost of buying materials,

products directly used to create the service.

The cost of sales does not include any

general and administrative expenses.

+

Overheads

Rent, electricity, travel…

+

Profit Margin

As a business, every decision must be made on purpose. Here are two pricing strategies that work well for the HBI depending on your business model:

PRESTIGE PRICING STRATEGY

This strategy is based on high pricing, showing that your services are high value, luxury, and premium. It will focus on the perceived value rather than the cost of it. When we talk about 'high,' it is relative to what you do and your competitors' prices. It is all about what makes the experience special. Do you offer bubbly with any service? Does your client get a nice head massage? Are you working one-on-one? Is the area where you work elite? Once again, experience is all about details and added value.

PSYCHOLOGICAL PRICING STRATEGY

The secret is in the price list. First, you will set it so that high prices are close to lower prices; offer bundled and psychological prices such as £99.99.

Bundled prices and offers can be exceedingly catchy; it en courages the client to get more for a little less.

For example:

Eyebrow shape: £15.00

Eyebrow tint: £15.00

Eyebrow shape + tint: £27.99

Both techniques are not targeting the same client type; what pricing strategy would suit your client?

Honestly, setting prices can be challenging and frustrating. Sometimes we don't feel worthy or struggle to realise the value of our skills. We might doubt our experience or not feel as qualified as others and get stuck comparing ourselves (especially on social media!) If you feel this way at any stage of your business, remember that people are ready to pay to benefit from your talents and expertise.

The time will come for you to review your costs and analyse their impact on your profitability, and you may want to adjust your price list. You might also decide to review your price list, maybe because of cost increase or high demand, and if you did not set the correct prices right away, you will be given a second chance.

Whatever strategy you choose, make sure to practice clear and fair rates—the more transparent you are, the more your clients will understand! It's a win-win situation, you will obtain the profit you desired, and your clients will keep coming to you because they truly see and believe the value of your services.

Notes about pricing

PART 8

Useful apps

Work smarter, not harder!

Apps can be so practical—with the right apps, you can do much more in less time. But, as you know, the market offers so many apps, and it can quickly get confusing as to which ones to choose since there's an app for almost everything. Be careful—it can also get too complex and way too expensive if you get too many of them!

I used to know a mobile colourist who travelled from house to house with the future of his business in a tiny notebook: all his client details, addresses, colour recipes, etc. Imagine if he misplaced his notebook or dropped a coffee on it: he would have lost everything. Customer DATA for a business it is gold; not to mention that legally you must protect it, as you are responsible for it.

There are many apps on the market, and depending on what you need, you can work with one only or combine a few—from managing your stock to an accounting or booking app: you can choose!

When buying an app, read the reviews to get an accurate idea of what current users are thinking—some apps are full of bugs! And do not forget to double-check the monthly fees.

Here are two of my favourite app types

Accounting app

Tracks my financial situation—I can make invoices, estimates, track stats on my income, expenses, bank account balances, tax estimations, stock, and so on. Money always needs good management, and an accounting app should help you stay in charge of your finances and support you in decision making.

It's imperative to me to keep a good overview of my freelancing business' financial situation.

When starting your business, you may not know how to create an invoice and wonder what the legal requirements in your country are. Most of the time, these apps are user-friendly and often offer free support and training included in your plan.

Booking app

Helps me with my bookings and saves me so much time! It keeps data of my clients; my customers can book themselves at any time on their own. It also keeps the appointment records, sends reminders to clients, and much more.

When you are working on your own, it is a game-changer!

Banking app, contact management app, stock management app, invoicing app—the choice is extensive, and it blows my mind that you can access your data from your phone— anywhere you go!

A great app is focused, intuitive, fast, and a pleasure to use. When choosing apps, here is what you may want to ask yourself:

BRAINSTORM

- What assistance do I need?
- What would make my life easier?
- What do I need to track?
- How much will it cost me/is it worth the investment?

A good app will generally

- Be easy to use
- Save you time and money
- Have good reviews
- Not have too many features to avoid bugs
- Great customer service

Here are some well-known apps that may be worth a look:

COCONUT

QUICKBOOKS

ZERVANT

XERO

SAGE ONE

ACUITY SCHEDULING

SQUARESPACE

ZAPIER

SIMPLYBOOK ME

It's all about how you have decided to work.

Do your research considering the business model you are choosing, and the choice is yours!

Notes about apps

PART 8

ACCOUNTANT

A professional accountant is not compulsory but is highly recommended. Due to how we operate, a freelance hair or beauty
expert has a lot to learn and do regarding financial management. Without basic accounting skills, your business' finances
may not survive.

If you are doing this for the very first time, you will be smart to
have somebody to talk to; an adviser when legal requirements
change, or if you are ever struggling with money.
You will benefit from professional advice from somebody who
knows your business and the complexity of your accounts.
A business is not a long and quiet river. You could end up in
a situation where you will need extra help. Make sure a professional has your back (which is better than Googling info
that you don't understand). Life happens, a world pandemic
could happen, and you could end up with financial issues...
who knows!

Also, when you are self-employed or a freelancer, it can be
tricky to get a mortgage. Usually, banks or other companies
ask for 2–3 years' worth of accounts, so you better have clean
and professionally managed accounts to present.

An accountant will also save you money and help you to establish a financial strategy. For example, they will explain to you what is deductible or not or if you need to register for VAT.

A good accountant will be one of your best investments. When looking for the right one, make sure you get along; they must explain professional jargon, making it simplified and easy to understand. Make sure you can afford them too!

When I built my first company in the UK, I did not speak English, so I chose to work with a French accountant firm in London. I had not planned to spend so much money on accounting services, which seriously impacted my cash flow. I learned something: there are always unexpected expenses.

Being thrifty at the beginning can buy you more flexibility with your budget when needed. It's a real game-changer, even if it is not always possible.

Some of the basic accounting skills for a freelance HBI expert include:

TRACKING EVERY TRANSACTION

As a freelancer, you are typically not directly accountable to a boss. However, you are totally in charge of how you spend your income, and you know how dicey that can be.

Just because you are not necessarily reporting your expenses to anyone does not mean you should care less about documenting your transactions. And you will agree with me that it's way easier to note significant expenses than lesser ones. But the truth is, tiny drops of water make an ocean, and so do little expenses accumulate to enormous amounts.

Get a jotter, diary, or anything that can help you keep records. Document every detail of money flow—both in and out. That way, you will know when you start spending on things that don't weigh much on the scale of priority.

Some costs you should consciously take note of and properly document include:

- Expenses on mobile phone
- Internet services for business
- Travel expenses
- Purchase invoices
- Education
- Business development materials

SET ASIDE MONEY

If you work with an employer, you probably will have a fixed way of getting paid. That way, you know exactly when to expect money, so you plan your expenses into that time.

But as a freelancer, there's most likely no rule over how and when money flows in unless you make one for yourself. As a result, you may not be totally in charge of when work comes to you as a freelancer.

The adverse effect is that your spending may not be as structured as it should be. And it means there's no guarantee you will settle first things first.

To curb this, learn to set money aside for every significant expense. Tax, for instance, can attract financial penalties if it's not duly settled. So, it is best to allocate funds to such expenses to avoid forgetting or neglecting them later.

Separate Business Funds from Personal Money

Most of the time, this is not as easy as it sounds. With regular employment, you can clearly distinguish between the company's money and your own. But when you are working for yourself, it's a different game entirely.

As a freelancer, you must make deliberate efforts to distinguish between your business' funds and personal money. It starts with keeping an accurate record of transactions, carefully noting those directly for business.

It is not necessarily limited to just finances; it applies to assets too. For example, using personal properties for freelance business and vice versa may be helpful if you're just starting. But it only increases the chances of making an overlap between personal and business resources as your business grows.

Get a Separate Account for Business

It is also highly recommended that you get a business account apart from your personal account. It usually solves the issue of money all flowing into and out of one source, which may be confusing at some point.

Your business account statement will be able to give a clear report of what exactly came in or left your business. One of the next topics is bank accounts. Keep reading and learn more about your options.

Notes about accountant

FREELANCER

Bank account

It's imperative to keep a good overview of your freelancing business' financial situation.

While a business bank account is not compulsory and legally required for freelancers in every country, a business bank account is more likely to help you manage your money and save time. You will use it for transactions to receive money from your clients, pay yourself, pay for taxes, and work expenses. A business bank account is like a personal bank account. It will assist you better in tracking your business expenses, look more professional, and simplify your business accounting.

A business bank account will ultimately help you manage your cash flow. Cash flow is the total amount of cash that moves in and out of business. It is simply a record of the amount received by the company and the amount spent by the business.

With accurate information about your cash flow, you can quickly figure out when your business is spending more than it is earning. Your cash flow helps you trace expenses that can be avoided or that are unnecessary.

Choosing a bank is a crucial point. But, first, you must do some research. Many options are available on the market, especially since online banking is competing with high street banking. Again, there is no 'best' choice; you need to consider your business needs and carefully compare all options when choosing a bank.

BRAINSTORM

- How to contact your bank if you seek assistance?
- Are there any interest rates?
- What documents/references are needed?
- Do they provide further services?
- Do you need multi-currency accounts?
- Pricing: account opening and transaction fees?
- Can you make a deposit?
- Do you get a bank card?
- Cost of replacement card?

Online banking has become quite popular for freelancers and small businesses. They offer accounts for freelancers, which sometimes include built-in accounting and tax solutions and other features that you may want to compare.

While high street banks and online banks have both pros and cons, they might differ. Below are a few examples:

ONLINE BANKING

Pros	Cons
Fast and easy to open (online).	Different types of regulations: make sure your money is protected.
Access to your account from anywhere – useful when you are traveling a lot.	No physical presence (branches).
Debit card.	Not all offer deposit options and overdrafts.
Send and receive payments.	Often a balance limit.

HIGH STREET BANKING

Pros	Cons
Branch: just walk in if you need to.	Higher fees.
Support: seek help in person.	Opening an account can take longer.
Wide range of services: overdrafts, insurances, card machine . . .	

When I set up a business bank account for my freelance company, I chose to do it with the bank I use for my personal bank accounts. So, I connected via my account and applied for a business account which was approved in a week. So far, I am pleased with the service.

Again, do what's best for you and your money.

Notes about bank account

_____

_____

_____

_____

_____

_____

_____

_____

_____

_____

_____

_____

_____

_____

_____

_____

_____

_____

_____

_____

_____

FREELANCER

PAYMENT METHODS

You will need to decide what payment facilities you want to offer your clients: bank transfer, card payment, cash, cheque, and others.

The most beneficial and straightforward payment method is bank card; it is a personal opinion, but I think it is effortless for your customers and looks very professional.

Cash is not my favourite payment method, but it absolutely remains a suitable option. It is again a personal opinion; however, as a freelancer, you are working alone, meaning that time management is critical and cashing up takes time. Not to mention that carrying some money to the bank is time-consuming and not always safe; a considerable amount of cash in your handbag is never a good idea.

There are also bank transfers, but I tend to think they are not always convenient. It can be time-consuming for the client to transfer the money to you just after the service—especially if they don't have your bank details registered already; on top of this, you'll need to connect to your bank account or banking app to check that the payment has arrived.
Even though bank transfers are more convenient for deposits, they remain an option.

For payments, my go-to is the card machine.

Nowadays, there is such a wide choice of card machines on the market—easy to use, no hidden fees, and a hassle-free feeling. It's life-changing for freelancers and small businesses— Sum up, iZettle, Square, PayPal —you name it!

Notes about payment methods

FREELANCER

INSURANCE

Why insure your business? Because stuff happens!
Working for yourself and being your own boss means that there is nobody to cover you. If you don't cover yourself, you could be liable to pay for unexpected damages, loss of legal fees, and accidental injury to a client.

It is crucial always to take precautions when performing any work, particularly if you use chemicals. Make sure you always strictly follow the instructions.

The harsh reality is that sometimes it just happens.
For example, a colour stain on a pair of £300 jeans, an allergic reaction to a product, maybe you accidentally spill some coffee on an immaculate white Dior bag, or (OMG!) there is a missing coat from the cloakroom!
Do you get it? Yes, you do.

In addition, sometimes, we just get tricky and complicated clients. There is no shame, and it's not a secret; we all get unhappy clients. However, we also get the recurring unhappy clients; they are the ones you cannot satisfy as they are generally unhappy in life. They will most of the time change their mind between the consultation and the end of the service. "Unhappy clients" will be dissatisfied and expect a "free fix," which will lead to a direct loss of revenue. Then there are also the "bad clients," the angry ones, who will be unfair and unreasonable. They often make you feel overwhelmed because it is hard to communicate with them; they complain about the prices, harass you with calls and emails, and have unrealistic expectations. This situation can lead to legal entanglements, loss of money, and even damage your relationships with other clients.

Always protect your back and follow your instinct. If it feels wrong, it probably is. If you have a terrible feeling, make sure the service is spot on, master your consultation, be honest and realistic about the service you are about to provide. Do not hesitate to make an estimate detailing the full-service scope and make sure the client agrees in writing. You must highlight any concern or essential point. The longer you're in business, the better you'll get at spotting them and NOT working with them, but if bad stuff happens; make sure you've got insurance to cover your back. When choosing insurance, you must assess your business to evaluate where the risks are and where you need cover.

You may want to look at and discuss all aspects with your potential insurance:

- Public liability
- Product liability

- Treatment risks
- Malpractice cover
- Financial loss
- Stock equipment insurance
- Legal expenses cover
- Personal accident cover

Also, do not forget to ask questions and read all the fine print!

Notes about insurance

PART 8

SUPPLIERS

Choose your suppliers wisely! It will save you time, money, and problems. As a freelancer, you are free to choose your suppliers; you can work with as many as you want—it is totally up to you. As much as we like word of mouth, do not hesitate to do your research. Social media, well-known brands, online searches—there is a lot of competition out there. Use it to your advantage.

Ideally, you want to work with your favourite supplies and products and build a stable and long-lasting relationship with your suppliers.

BRAINSTORM

- Will you need a big order to open an account?
- Are prices competitive?
- Delivery: lead time and shipping costs
- Social responsibility: do they supply safe supplies/ products (especially chemicals)?
- Convenience: any benefits? For example, online orders?
- Risk: can they consistently see demand?
- Are they trade only? Or do they sell to the public?
- For how many years have they been trading?

- Distance: where are they geographically?

You might also want to check their reputation: do they have online reviews? I want to stress an important point about reviews: check the rating numbers, but make sure you read what people say without forgetting to check if the business answered. There are unfair and unrealistic clients everywhere; they could complain about something they already got compensation for, so if a company has bad reviews, make sure you understand them. If you are ready to take the plunge:

- Make a list of some products you will use and send it to a supplier and their competitors for comparison. You will be able to check their rates and determine how friendly and responsive they are.

- Select some suppliers and set up a meeting/call to understand their terms and conditions.

- Try to negotiate their rates if you can.

Notes about suppliers

Terms and conditions of business

A Terms & Conditions (T&C) agreement is essential for all businesses, including small businesses and freelancers.

It dictates the rules for your services and lays out expectations for you and your customers. But, again, it is your business; it is your responsibility to set the rules.

These agreements cover services, bookings, tardiness, skin tests, obligations, pricing, payment, intellectual property, confidentiality, liability, and more.

When creating a business, you are very busy and sometimes tend to put aside T&C; however, unnecessary disputes can often be avoided saving you from potentially bad-intentioned clients.

Who doesn't want peace of mind? Terms and conditions are the utmost part of any business for its appropriate regulation.

A business walks on a straight path when the business owners have set the directives. This document must be custom-made for you by a law professional to set straightforward terms to ensure that the customer is well aware of their services and knows what to expect.

A law professional will also advise you where to display your T&C depending on your country's regulations.

You could be tempted by searching some T&C online and simply copy and paste to save money. Please resist! Get a certified law professional on a freelancer platform to draft a bespoke document appropriate to your business.

This will give you peace of mind.

Notes about terms and conditions

_____

_____

_____

_____

_____

_____

_____

_____

_____

_____

_____

_____

_____

_____

_____

_____

_____

_____

_____

_____

_____

_____

PART 8

PROMOTE YOUR BRAND: STRATEGY

Promote your brand and get your business to take off! When I created my first company, I was selling nail services. My marketing strategy was to tell everybody around me that I had created a business providing nail services; basically, I just relied on word of mouth as a strategy. It is reliable (and my favourite), but it can take time for word to spread when you start a business from scratch.

So, I also bet on leaflets. I left 5,000 of them on the cars parked in the biggest shopping centre of my town - where by the way, my clientele type would have never been to. My friends and I spent days and nights doing this, and out of 5,000 leaflets, I made three new clients (and they were nothing like my ideal clients!)

In my defence, social media was not a thing yet - but still, what a waste of time and money!

Reflecting further, it was also such a waste of paper; I was not concerned about living more sustainably at that point. But we learn and grow, and this is a mistake I have never made again; I could not be more grateful for social media today.

As you can understand, it is about sharing the right message in the right place; this is when a clear and good-looking brand pays off. First, understand your customer journey is essential - you need to find out when and where they are connecting, then engage.

How are you going to promote your brand? Technology is a true asset. First, however, you need to consider your brand objective. To define who your customer/ audience is and where they are engaging from is a must.

FIVE TIPS TO BUILDING A MARKETING STRATEGY

1. MISSION STATEMENT

The first thing to do is to define your mission.
What is your mission statement? Ideally, you want to target an audience, contribute with a service or a product and explain how you make the difference.

Here is some inspiration for you, the mission statement of some leading brands:

Phyto

> "*For over 50 years, PHYTO has been a leader in plant-based hair care and salon-quality formulas. Our products embrace the principle that healthy hair begins at the root. Built on a heritage of craftsmanship and cutting-edge scientific advancements, PHYTO boasts the highest concentrations of pure plant extracts in today's beauty market. Our formulas are 95% natural overall with select products up to 100% natural. As one of the world's most respected hair care brands, PHYTO is recognised as a symbol of performance, expertise, and timeless beauty.*
>
> *POWERFUL HAIR CARE WITH PROVEN RESULTS BORN FROM OUR GENUINE LOVE AND RESPECT FOR NATURE.*"

Schwarzkopf Professional

"We are one. Bound together by our love of hair. We are fuelled by the same fire and devotion to our craft.

Our collective ambition to excel drives our spirit. To question. To explore. To outdo what's been done before.

And so, we create and recreate.

We refine and redesign.

We take what's been broken and rebuild.

We reshape and revive, repair, and restore.

We re-colour what has lost vibrancy and restyle what has lost its edge. We reveal what's been hidden and replace the old with the new.

Rethinking, reworking, renewing…

We are always… reinventing hair."

These are all powerful statements. Of course, they are leading brands, but don't forget that, as a small business, you are on a mission too.

What is your mission statement? What is at the core of what you do? Your mission does not have to be lengthy, it just needs to be catchy and true to your business.

2.Set your marketing goals

Goals are often the place to start. They will set the direction for what needs to happen for your product or service. The purpose of marketing is to reach your target audience and communicate the benefits of your product or service; so, you can successfully grow your clientele, sell your products, and develop your business.

What are your marketing goals? Here is some inspiration for you:

- Grow an email list
- Increase SM following
- Generate conversation rate
- Raise brand awareness
- Get more engagement on your website
- Increase customer value
- Rank higher in the search result
- Establish an authority within your industry
- Boost brand engagement
- Increase revenue
- Sell education
- Generate bookings
- Reach new clients

The list goes on and on; add your own marketing goals.

3.IDENTIFY WHAT YOU ARE SELLING

What you want to do is to go above and beyond the service or the product itself; you want to understand what people want to buy.

What do you sell?
Are you selling a haircut?

No! You are selling emotions. A haircut can lift someone's emotional state and mood by making them feel sexy and powerful; it gives a sense of being in control; as silly as it can seem, it can be such an achievement. A fresh haircut boosts one's confidence and self-esteem; it is not only about cutting hair.

Are you selling a spray tan service?
People don't want to buy a spray tan service; they want to buy a beautiful, radiant golden body on the beach.

Are you selling the latest hair keratin treatment?
People don't buy a hair keratin treatment; they buy the shiny and strong hair they always wanted.

<u>People are buying</u>

Promises

Benefits

Experiences

Stories

Relationships

Results

4. IDENTIFY YOUR AUDIENCE

Who are you selling to and why?

You need to identify a set of individual characteristics or needs that you hope to serve and fulfil. For example, what are their psychological factors: lifestyle, social status, activities? Where are they living? Most of the time, their typical profile will be your ideal client's profile— it is best to be as specific as possible and to include as much detail as possible.

For example: you are a balayage expert in New York City. Your target is women's state-of-the-art style. They are looking for low-maintenance and natural-looking hair. Their perfect colour for them is a seamless blonde balayage. They need to like and appreciate expensive-looking hair. They are between 30 and 55 years old. They are on-trend, hang around fancy places, perhaps in a specific area...

Who's your audience?

5. IDENTIFY HOW TO ENGAGE

How will you engage?

BRAINSTORM

- Will you use Google business? Will you ask for reviews?
- Will you use search engine optimisation (SEO)?
- Will you advertise yourself on a beauty app?
- Will you use social media? If yes, on what platforms?
- Will you create a mailing list?
- Will, you set up a blog?
- Will you pay for advertising ads? Google, Facebook…
- Will you brand your vehicle?
- Will you use affiliates to promote your service? Bloggers, digital influencers?
- Will you connect? Community, charities, associations?
- Will you partner up?
- Will you offer free consultations?
- Will you work on word of mouth?
- Will you donate a prize to a local fundraiser?
- Will you enter business awards/competitions?
- Will you create a customer loyalty scheme?
- Will you make a bespoke offer?
- Will you run a social media competition?
- Will you start a podcast?
- Will you hire a marketing consultant?
- Will you offer referral rewards?
- Will you set up a loyalty card system?

It is also essential to track and measure your marketing strategy. You can use software to assist you if necessary, such as Klipfolio or Google analytics. You will also need to decide on the channel you want to track, such as your website, social media, or referral. You will also need to determine what to measure, in other words, what you are interested to see as a result: bookings, page views, SM effectiveness...

Be creative; there are so many strategies out there! You can also ask for the help of a marketing strategist to start you off. A good marketing strategy is not always expensive. The truth is that it can be time-consuming, so building a marketing strategy that works for you is key.

Be organised and remember no pain, no gain!

Notes about marketing strategy

PART 8

SOCIAL MEDIA

It's not a secret anymore; social media is game-changing for businesses! Every single successful brand uses it—and for a good reason!

Like it or not, social media is the new way of connecting customers and businesses, and it is not likely to change anytime soon.

Social platforms are the natural places to promote your business. All you need is a chic business page to showcase you (remember, you are the brand), your incredible services, and your products.

Social media is a true asset to your business. But, talking about the HBI, on every single platform, thousands of local and international brands and industry superstars compete. So, it can be intimidating to dare to showcase your work too. But you know what? If treated correctly, social media platforms can be your best friend. It is essential to only stick to platforms that can benefit you in the long term.

> # Four platforms that could help any freelancer to grow their business:

1. Facebook

With over 2.7 billion monthly active users as of the second quarter of 2020, Facebook is the most extensive social network worldwide.

With time, apart from organic posts, you can also invest in Facebook Marketing to promote your services and products and increase your reach, engagements, and overall sales. In addition, Facebook has its native shops named "Facebook Shop," where you can create different catalogues, upload pictures, highlight offers, and more.

2. YouTube

YouTube can be an effective video platform for small businesses. It is not always straightforward, but you can gradually improve your social presence with proper planning and insightful content.

When filming, the image and audio quality is crucial; consider using software and good filming material. The initial in vestment time/cost can be high. However, depending on several factors, such as how often you plan to post videos, getting help from a professional to film/edit your content can be worth it.

Make it as professional as possible; your YouTube channel will be an integral part of your brand and need to represent your standards.

You can create tutorials on products that you sell, promote the client experience or a new service, you can upload long and short videos on this platform- and even longer videos if your account is verified!

Videos, in general, bring in the most engagement, as users prefer to see engaging content rather than looking at a static image. Make it enjoyable, professional, and as polished as possible.

3.INSTAGRAM

You don't need me to write statistics about how long people spend on this platform daily: more than necessary for sure, but good news, it is extra beneficial to your business! Instagram is a dynamic and valuable visual platform. It also provides numerous options to showcase your products and services.

You can build up a beautiful grid, share stories, reels, create and upload long videos and much more. It allows you to share your brand's story with millions of people.

An exciting story is a great way to create an emotional connection with your audience. Furthermore, Instagram marketing can be worth it—you can also invest some money to promote your profile.

This platform regularly offers new features, and the algorithm changes constantly; keep an eye on it to stay in the loop. It is a wise thing to do!

4. TikTok

Sometimes it's funny, sometimes it's cringy, but it's addictive! TikTok hasn't been just the fastest growing social media network of 2020, but of all time! It enables users to film and share short-form video content by utilising a vast range of features. The secret is to catch people's attention within the first seconds of the video. It can sound challenging, but if you make it, your video could go viral within a few hours!

> What a topic! Social media deserves a whole book
> on its own! But let's start you off with 5 top tips:

1.CHOOSE THE RIGHT PLATFORM(S) FOR YOU AND YOUR BUSINESS

Define where your clientele is, post quality content, and engage. As a small business, pick the right platform that works for you. If you decide to engage on many media platforms simultaneously, make sure it is not overwhelming as you must stay committed to it. Market your brand in front of billions of people worldwide instantly; it is all about understanding your client journey, where your audience/clients connect, what social platforms they use, and where their touch-points are.

2.EDUCATE YOURSELF ON SOCIAL MEDIA

It's an investment that will help you make money. You can do your research, but you also have the option to join social media classes. They will help you understand the technology of social media, such as algorithms that will maximise your chances of driving traffic to your page and build your community without burning out.

Long and short education programs are specifically designed for people within the HBI - a real asset for your business. They'll be talking your professional language, advising you on taking the right pictures, using the proper techniques and hashtags, and developing specific skills content. Building a consistent social media presence and turning followers into clients is massively important and will take some time, but hard work and consistency will pay off.

3.CREATE A PLAN

Creating your social media marketing strategy doesn't need to be painful! First, summarise everything you plan to do and hope to achieve on social media. It will guide your actions—the more specific your plan is, the more effective it will be.

4.USE APPS TO PLAN, CREATE AND EDIT YOUR CONTENT

Content planner apps can be truly life-changing! Most apps are designed to assist you with content creation, captions, posting, hashtags, analytics, and more; the goal is to simplify the process in an effective and quicker lapse of time. They will also help you create and plan flawless and on-brand content.

Some of the apps are even free, which is risk-less; give them a go!

5.CREATE BEAUTIFUL AND ON-BRAND CONTENT:

The HBI is very much about visual impact. One of the secrets of success on social media is posting appealing content. Make sure to get people's attention in a short period of 3 seconds; this is why beautiful content is essential to catch their attention.

Why not devote a day regularly to shoot social media content? You can work on models and create a stunning stockpile of photos and videos to plan your content and not feel overwhelmed with content creation during work. It will allow you to showcase - and ultimately sell - the kind of work you love. Attract the right clients!

Alternatively, creating content quickly while working takes training, but it is a habit that will help you to renew your content regularly. So, if you wonder what you can do to grow your community, target potential clients, and increase your sales, here are some of the social media hacks and tips that can help you out:

- Research your competitors.

Pinpoint the keywords you want to rank your products/ services for (you can use Google Keywords Planner for this - it is a free tool).

- Study your target audience based on your ideal client: their age, gender, behaviours, preferences, interests, and other demographics.

- Decide on your targeting areas: if you sell a service, it will be around you, but products can be shipped.

- Perform a social media audit of your favourite accounts doing similar things as you; check what content they share, what offers they promote, what kind of followers they have on their Instagram handles, etc.

- Create a social media calendar and list down several posts you want to publish per week. Why not start with at least two posts per week?

- Inspect Instagram and Facebook stories, re-share your pictures, tag local influencers. To get heard, use hashtags where the algorithm tells you to so that your profile becomes discoverable.

- Collaborate and communicate with local businesses to cre- ate long-term human-centric relationships and connect with local people. Creating and maintaining connections and collaborations will allow you to create a community of loyal customers, partners, and followers.

- Be honest, authentic, and transparent with your content. Do not use filters that could set unrealistic expectations for your clients. For example, if you are a facialist selling a treatment to embellish the skin, you will probably post a before/after pictures—do not apply a filter to smooth down the skin even more as your next client will expect this same result on their skin too.

- Engage personally with your audience through comments or direct messages as often as you can.

Not all social platforms are alike but let me say it, quality over quantity. It's not about having 10k followers who don't engage and communicate on your brand's pages. It is about having genuine followers/people on your brand's social profiles who engage and connect. It doesn't matter if they are 100 or 1,000 in counting.

A few years ago, during a business trip in Brazil, I visited a salon in the chic area of Sao Paulo. After 2 minutes of talk, the assistants asked me to follow their business profile on instagram. Later, they explained how pressurised they were feeling about followers on Instagram - to them, if your following was low, then you were not a good hairdresser. Quick and vital reminder: some businesses make millions and don't even have 1,000 real followers, so do not let a number define you as a hair or beauty expert.

Remember, you are doing this for your business; to build a clientele. You are not doing it for the fame or the significant number at the top of your profile—unless your goal is to monetise your profile, which is another topic altogether!

Create workable strategies. By frequently optimising your social media strategies for each platform, you will maintain the flow of engagement on your business profiles. And when we talk about social media strategy, consistent communication through content should be the top priority!

Why not contact a social media strategist freelancer to benefit from professional advice and extra guidance?

Pick the platform (or platforms) that works for you, create, commit, and rock it!

notes about social media

PART 8

FINAL THOUGHTS

BECOMING A FREELANCER and taking the leap can be such an exciting adventure, but you must make sure you are ready. Timing is very crucial and calculating all the factors to make your small business succeed is vital! As a freelancer, you will have access to unlimited opportunities if you keep your eyes peeled.

Connect, engage, and take action. You will learn and grow in a way you haven't imagined before because this is what happens when we make a move!

There will be days when you will feel that things are not working out in your favour; however, there will be a time when you thank yourself for not quitting.

Patience is the key to success.

There are a thousand ways to make your business stand out, and I am confident that you will find yours. You are unique, and your uniqueness will attract the right clientele for you. The competition is high, but do not forget that nobody is you. Trust yourself and believe in yourself; stand for your standards as much as your values.

Take your business seriously. It's not because you are a small business that you are insignificant; act as if you are big, tell the world out loud that you exist, and please make a tremendous impact.

Nobody knows what tomorrow will bring. Both times when I started as a freelancer, I liked to carefully assess the risk factors— "what if it does not work?" "what do I have to lose?" or "if I fail, what is my plan B?" I always came up with the thought that many entrepreneurs try so many times before becoming successful; there will always be a plan B or a second chance. Failure has never been an option with any of my businesses, but in the end, why not?

When I decided to close my first business, it did feel like a massive failure, even if it was for an exciting opportunity.

From another perspective, the absolute failure would have been not trying; I learned so much on the way, met incredible people, and it gave me the priceless privilege of the experience.

As I once did, you might sometimes feel bitter-sweet about your previous experiences in salons and may hold on to some hard feelings. But whatever happened in the past, good, or bad, it is necessary to accept and move on. I believe that bad experiences particularly shape us and make us the strong professionals and humans we are today when we overcome potential anger and regrets.

When you know that you are ready to start your own business with a great business plan as evidence, I think that not doing it could lead to regrets; to me, there is just nothing worse!

To be alone is a choice, and it is not the freelancer fatality. However, you will quickly understand that being surrounded by inspiring and loving people is game-changing and will help you make the right choices for your business.

In my case, taking the leap and becoming a freelancer felt right the second time; I knew I was ready, I had a small client base, and could self-fund my project. I was determined.

Becoming a freelancer benefitted my life a lot; by choosing this lifestyle, I am choosing to prioritise myself and every time I work hard, it is a good investment that pays off.

Reflecting on my journey, I have never had as much flexibility; my life feels more balanced and healthier than ever.

Professionally, freedom is liberating! Being able to accept any opportunity contributes to diversifying my work and allows me to widen my network.

Understanding client archetype is essential. It helps me pick the right clients for me and my business. I feel happy at work. It comforts me in my lifestyle choice and makes me love my business even more.

Time taught me not to work with anybody, and I always go with my gut; just follow your instinct.

Being a freelancer, I am totally in control of my career. Running a business that you have built from scratch is extremely powerful and feels like an incredible achievement.

But ultimately, the thing that pushed me to do it was that I could finally provide the service I wanted to provide to my clients. I control the client experience from A–Z; I can finally work one-on-one and the appreciation from my customer is just so heart-warming and rewarding: I am in love with my job again.

After you've read this book, if you think freelancing is for you, give it a go, draw up a business plan and if it makes sense to start the adventure, do it!

Like anything in life, there are always inconveniences, but the advantages are so unarguably worth it. To be free, healthy, and happy at work is so powerful and satisfying.

Even with a small clientele, you can always find a way to increase your income by marketing yourself better, upgrading your service menu, or offering a new retail product. Making more money does not always mean working more. Using motivation and creativity to drive your business is key. Money should never be your "why" when creating a business as it needs to be deeper than this, but quite frankly, any successful freelancer of the HBI will tell you, "work less, earn more" and it is not a myth. You are the one deciding whether you are going to get the money you deserve. It means complete control of your income. So, let's work smarter, not harder!

To be a freelancer right now is just perfect for me. I have no idea if I will be a freelancer for the rest of my life; we grow, change, and opportunities show up.

Secretly, I'd love to live and work in between 2 countries, but for now, I embrace life as it is—I am a FREELANCER, and I feel FULFILLED and FREE.

I hope this book has provided you with all the guidance and inspiration you needed. Now, my question for you is:

Are you going to take the leap?

ACKNOWLEDGEMENTS

THANK YOU TO everyone who made it possible.

I would have never thought that writing a book would be such an adventure. I started writing during the 2020-2021 lock-down; it kept me sane, and the hope that it could help people of my industry brightened my days. I've written it with love, passion, and determination.

Of course, I could have never done it without the help and support from the people surrounding me.

Special thanks to Ieva.S, my ride or die friend; Ludo, my partner and business partner, Lacey Hunter-Felton co-founder of Hunter Collective, and thanks to you mum and dad for being such an inspiration; when you look at me, I feel I can reach the stars.

BIBLIOGRAPHY &
USEFUL RESOURCES

National Hair & Beauty Federation:
www.nhbf.co.uk

Start-Up Donut (Financing a Business):
www.startupdonut.co.uk.

The Brand Stylist:
www.thebrand-stylist.com

Dummies (Accounting Cheat Sheet):
www.dummies.com

The Entrepreneur Handbook (How to Promote your Business:)
www.entrepreneurhandbook.co.uk

UpWork:
www.upwork.com

PHYTO Haircare:
www.phyto-haircare.co.uk

Schwarzkopf:
www.schwarzkopf-professionalusa.com

Freelancing | Prospects.ac.uk.
https://www.prospects.ac.uk/jobs-and-work-experience/self-employment/freelancing

Printed in Great Britain
by Amazon

78611003R00129